If your church is even thinking about star
(or has one already), this book should be requ
connects the dots between church history,
thought about online spiritual community.
every question (and no book could, given th
matter), it goes a long way toward resolving t
"real"? As an internet campus pastor, I think th
what it will be. A worthwhile read for anyone
and real connection in the virtual world.

—BRIAN VASIL
INTERNET CAMPUS PASTOR
FLAMINGO ROAD CHURCH

Christian theology has yet to take full stock of the emergence of virtual worlds together with its promises and perils for the church. Douglas Estes challenges entrenched ways of thinking about what it means to be the church in light of his positive assessment of virtual congregations. While this book makes some controversial points, at the very least it raises provocative questions as it attempts to shift the burden of proof to the defenders of traditional models of church.

—ADONIS VIDU, PHD
ASSOCIATE PROFESSOR OF THEOLOGY
GORDON-CONWELL THEOLOGICAL SEMINARY

D0051297

SimChurch

Being the Church
in the Virtual World

DOUGLAS ESTES

ZONDERVAN.com/
AUTHOR**TRACKER**
follow your favorite authors

We want to hear from you. Please send your comments about this book to us in care of zreview@zondervan.com. Thank you.

ZONDERVAN

SimChurch
Copyright © 2009 by Douglas Charles Estes

This title is also available as a Zondervan ebook.
Visit www.zondervan.com/ebooks.

This title is also available in a Zondervan audio edition.
Visit www.zondervan.fm.

Requests for information should be addressed to:

Zondervan, *Grand Rapids, Michigan 49530*

Library of Congress Cataloging-in-Publication Data

Estes, Douglas.
    SimChurch : being the church in the virtual world / Douglas C. Estes.
        p.   cm.
    Includes bibliographical references.
    ISBN 978-0-310-28784-1 (softcover)
    1. Church. 2. Technology — Religious aspects — Christianity. 3. Virtual reality — Religious aspects — Christianity. 4. Christianity and culture. I. Title.
    BV600.3.E88   2009
    262.00285 — dc22   2009009946

Interior design by Melissa Elenbaas

Printed in the United States of America

---

09 10 11 12 13 14 15 • 22 21 20 19 18 17 16 15 14 13 12 11 10 9 8 7 6 5 4 3 2 1

for Wyatt

Contents

Foreword

Come As You Are,
Just Put Some Clothes On!

A few years ago, I experienced a ministry "first." Someone walked into our lobby nude. She sat down in a chair in front of several other people in the lobby and did not speak to anyone. I received a phone call from a volunteer explaining all of this. I got there as soon as I could, and sure enough, there she was, completely naked sitting in our LifeChurch.tv lobby!

I politely asked her to put some clothes on and told her that she was welcome here, but that she would need to cover up. She continued to sit quietly with no response. I once again asked her to cover up, but she simply refused and did not answer. I then told her that she would have to leave and quickly removed her from the property.

Now ... all of this happened in our virtual campus on Second Life. We opened our doors there in March 2007 and have since welcomed visitors from all over the world.

After ejecting the naked lady, I began to wonder if I did the right thing. We often say we don't have a dress code, but in that moment I realized we do! I probably would have responded differently if she simply had said something in response. We have rules on the island, and it is clearly listed as a place that does not allow "mature" (adult) content. I took her silence as defiance and an unwillingness to listen. Maybe I was right; maybe I was wrong. But no matter how we handle situations like this, we can be assured that ministry in online and virtual environments presents some new and interesting challenges.

What Does This Mean for the Church?

Over the last one hundred years, technology has influenced nearly every culture on the planet.

A farmer in an African village can now get prices on his grain by using his mobile phone.

Grandparents in India can see and talk to their grandchildren in America through a video chat that costs nothing.

A church leader in an urban area of the UK can share ideas and resources with a pastor in Australia, transferring files and exchanging emails in seconds.

In our lifetime, technology has transformed not only the way we communicate but also the context in which we communicate. We find ourselves faced with a steady stream of new methods for interacting with each other — new tools and even new environments.

In fact, today, interactions have expanded beyond the physical realm into virtual worlds like Second Life and Metaverse. Though it's still debated by some, one could argue that these new methods of interaction have created new opportunities for community to take place.

As we experience community online and connect in virtual worlds like Second Life, we're redefining relationships and what they mean in society, business, politics, and the church.

As a pastor, I'm often evaluating the implications of online and virtual-world interaction for the church. Should we engage in these new environments? And if so, how? With the rapid pace of change that's taking place globally, we're at an ideal moment in history for the church to ask these questions and explore the opportunities that arise from new developments.

At LifeChurch.tv, we've been considering these questions prayerfully. We're coming to our own conclusions, putting solutions in place, and continuing to ask more questions as we move forward. Many churches around the world are embarking on this process, wrestling with their responses and what they mean for reaching their communities.

In *SimChurch*, Douglas Estes takes on these important questions and provides the framework to help us arrive at our own answers. What does the Bible say about virtual church? What can we learn about this issue from church history? How do we address the sacraments, baptism, and other church traditions in these virtual worlds?

Estes goes beyond just posing these questions and explores real-life examples of what ministries are currently doing, how they're working, and what it all means in the context of Scripture. Along the way, he helps us develop a common language so the conversation can be appropriately discussed.

Whether you're a tech expert or a skeptic, *SimChurch* does a masterful job of bringing everyone into this important conversation. Regardless of where you find yourself on these issues, it's critical we ask ourselves what online community and virtual environments can mean for our churches. Step into *SimChurch* and begin exploring new dimensions of ministry.

— BOBBY GRUENEWALD,
LIFECHURCH.TV PASTOR,
INNOVATION LEADER

Preface

Virtual churches are happening. Many of us have heard of virtual churches or read some news reports about them but have never really ventured into their world. Up to now, most studies of virtual churches have been from a limited, ethnographic, social-scientific perspective — who they are, what types of people they are reaching, how people feel about them. That's great, but what about the theology and ecclesiology of virtual churches? What do they believe about doing church and being the church? Will virtual churches change the way we do church in the real world? Is worship the same at an internet campus as it is at a real-world church? Can you even have a real church on the internet? There are a thousand and one questions we could ask.

Let's ask some thoughtful questions. It seems that many people talking about online ministry are either wide-eyed digitopians — the internet will create a new utopia — or wide-eyed alarmists — the internet is the source of all sin.[1] Sorry, but what the church at large needs is more measured, less sensational, deeper dialog on the merits and demerits of virtual churches. This book is a small step in that direction. A glance at Amazon.com reviews of books about the virtual world reveals that the number-one criticism is that books on virtual worlds are often fluff pieces — pretty pictures, nice ideas, but little substance. My goal was to do otherwise — to struggle with some deeper issues and keep prediction and speculation to a minimum.

Writing this book opened a huge can of worms for me. How can I talk about theology and ecclesiology in the virtual world when there are so many real-world groups at odds over these very things? Much of the work on ecclesiology in the last century has been so faddish you'd think it was a fashion show for churches.[2] In the end, even as I tried to write in generalities that are accessible to Christians of different stripes, I did what others more astute in ecclesiology than me also have done and felt was best: take a general position so as to ground the discussion.[3] Since I am committed to the Free Church model, this perspective underlies my work. Similar to Hans Küng, my goal in writing this book on an unusual area of theology is "to combine catholicity, a breadth and awareness of tensions, with evangelical concentration."[4]

To accomplish this, I have kept the discussion brief, especially when it concerns historical ecclesiology and philosophy. Both of these areas could contribute greatly to this discussion, but the book would be much more dense and less accessible to the average reader. In several places, I have tried to hint at some of the great underlying areas of philosophy and theology and how they affect our reasoning about a new form of church. Beyond this, my hope is that this book will generate more of these kinds of discussions at all levels. I suspect not only that what we learn about church in the virtual world will influence real-world churches but also that what we learn about people in the virtual world will help to shape how we perceive people in the real world.

Even after writing this book, I have more questions than answers. Let's ask questions together that will lead to healthier churches in every world.

Every book generates questions, this one more than most. Thanks to everyone who was willing to dialog with me about virtual churches and to wrestle with these issues. Special thanks go to Mark Brown (Anglican Cathedral), Pam Smith (i-church and St. Pixels), Bobby Gruenewald (LifeChurch.tv), and Brian Vasil (Flamingo Road) — all the strongest of pioneers. Thanks also to Tim Hutchings, Bill Chastain, John Hammett, Andrew "Tall Skinny Kiwi" Jones, Andrew Careaga, and Tim Challies, as well as everyone else who was involved in the conversation.

Great appreciation also goes to all of the wonderful people at Zondervan who care about the church in its every form for green-lighting this project, especially my editor, David Frees.

Finally, I'd like to thank all the awesome people at my church in the real world, Berryessa Valley Church; plus Damon Davenport and the folks at BuildtheVillage.org; Brandon Merrick at Christ the Life Lutheran Church; Gary Tuck, the staff, and my students at Western Seminary; Trevor van Laar; Brian Phipps and Chris Fann at Zondervan; Brandon Donaldson at LifeChurch.tv; Scott Swain; Mike and Juanita Lewis; Gary and Mary Appel; Rex Shipman; Scott and Jessica Brookshire; EGI Hosting; Lillie Boothe; Jason Woods; Ken Mears; Mark Howe; Scot McKnight; Chuck and Marivic Mora; Jason Estes; Eric Estes; Douglas R. Estes Jr.; and the rest of my extended family. Greatest thanks to my mom, Nadine, and above all to my wife, Noël, son, Wyatt, and daughter, Bridget — *Mungu wabariki sana*!

Hermas knew today's Sabbath would be different.

At least, he thought it would be. It started out as it always had—Rhoda preparing the children for worship at synagogue, arranging for the servants to come to synagogue services too, spending cherished moments of family time that the freedom of the Sabbath day allowed. As the time for synagogue came, Hermas and his family left the gate of their home and stepped onto the worn city streets of their hometown of Iconium.

It was the familiarity of the streets lined with apricot trees outside his house that caused Hermas' mind to wander ahead to synagogue. How many times had he walked the same streets to hear the Scriptures read during services? How many times had he found comfort during times of hardship in the close-knit community of his synagogue?

Yet today was different. They were not going to synagogue; they were going to the house of Euthalia, to a gathering called a church.

Hermas remembered how it all had started several months ago. Two foreign Jews had shown up at another synagogue in Iconium and started teaching, but teaching about "the Way," rather than simply instructing from the Torah. It caused a great furor, and the attendant of the scrolls got into a shouting match with one of those Jews. Within a week, the marketplace was abuzz with talk of the Way, of the true Messiah, of God's movement in the world. Hermas remembered the day Rhoda came home from market so excited, so joyous. A foreign Jew named Barnabas had been in the market teaching of the Way, and Rhoda had come to believe. She wanted Hermas and the family to observe the Sabbath at the church at Euthalia's house. Hermas had grudgingly agreed.

He had more than a few concerns. What would this "church" be like? Hermas could feel the grandeur of his God while sitting in the shadow of the columns of his synagogue, occasionally peeking out over the roofs of the nearby houses from the elevated and sacred site, but what grandeur would there be in a house? He could sense a connection with the ancient fathers when the ruler of the synagogue read from the Torah in the synagogue, but what connection would there be with God in this new church?

Quickly they arrived at Euthalia's, and so Hermas had to stow his fears and concerns. At the gate, several friends from their old synagogue greeted Hermas and his family, each radiating warmth and friendship. They entered the house. A new community for the people of God had begun.

chapter 1

Church in the Virtual World

Today a new community of the people of God has begun. We won't find it on the streets of our cities. Many of us won't even recognize it as a church. We all know churches — some are traditional, some are modern, some are mega, and some are emergent. For all of their apparent differences, each of these churches is basically the same — variations on the physical church in the modern era.[1] Partisans of one of the thirty-two flavors of modern churches may protest, but at the end of the day, they all belong to similar faith communities in the real world. Each one has a building with a front door that you open; each one has people who shake your hand; each one has pastors, ministers, elders, or leaders who proclaim God's Word to you; each one is real, tangible, physically present. There are differences, but there are more similarities.

A change is occurring in the Christian church the likes of which has not happened for centuries. At the beginning of the twenty-first century, the church is beginning to be different not in style, venue, feel, or volume but in the world in which it exists. A new gathering of believers is emerging, a church not in the real world of bricks and mortar but in the virtual world of IP addresses and shared experiences. This type of church is unlike any church the world has ever seen. It has the power to break down social barriers, unite believers from all over the world, and build the kingdom of God with a widow's mite of financing. It is a completely different type of church from any the world has ever seen.

Annus Virtualis

We are all familiar with the internet, or cyberspace. The internet exploded onto the scene in the last decade of the twentieth century. Cyberprophets predicted the end of the world as we knew it, a prediction that proved to be inaccurate. The real world is here to stay, though the internet remains a large part of our collective society. What happened? These cyberprophets misunderstood the nature of the explosion. As with all revolutionary advances, there is a period of uncertainty and exploration immediately followed by a time of adjustment. For example, even though Nikola Tesla invented the radio in the early 1890s, it was almost forty years before the world really figured out how to use it.[2] The same is true of the internet; even though the internet is a creation of the twentieth century, we will be well into the twenty-first century before our world comprehends and fully utilizes its capacity.

Already the internet is a mighty force. In 2007, the number of internet users passed one billion for the first time.[3] While this is only a little more than 20 percent of the world's population, at no other time in history since the time of Genesis has more than 20 percent of the world's population been in direct communication with each other. This statistic alone is theologically sobering. E-commerce has also kept up with the internet population boom; more than two trillion dollars changed hands over the internet in 2007.[4] Only a few years ago, booksellers sold 100 percent of their books in retail stores, but today more than 33 percent of all books sold are sold online.[5]

This is but the tip of the iceberg. In the early days of the internet, elementary applications such as email and bulletin board systems were the norm. These early applications seemed transformative, but they harnessed only a very small percentage of the power of the internet. Today a new wave of experiences — from self-published digital content to blogs to wikis to MMOGs[6] — has antiquated those early applications and pushed the internet one step closer to the day when the world will realize its full cybercapacity. If someone told you in 1980 that you could create your own movie or write your own book and sell it in a store that serves thirty million people, without the help of publishers, studios, lawyers, or marketers, you would have said they were crazy.[7] Now it's possible.

These new applications are only the second wave of the virtual tsunami that is transforming our world.[8] To grasp the magnitude of what is happening, it is vital that we see the internet not as a technological tool but as a paradigm shift in the way the world interacts on a fundamental level.[9] For example, you could look at a mobile phone as a technological tool — a telephone with no wires. Yet to do so misses the point. The mobile phone is a small paradigm shift in our world because it makes us no longer inaccessible. With the mobile phone, family, friends, colleagues, and solicitors can reach us in the car, in the theater, in the boardroom, or in the bathroom. The difference between the impact of the mobile phone and the internet is the magnitude of the shift: the internet is causing a paradigm shift a hundred times greater than that of the mobile phone.

We can see this shift already playing out in both the education and business worlds. Many US public schools now offer "virtual academies" for elementary schoolchildren. A student of higher education used to be forced to travel to attend an institution and to sit in a respected classroom in order to learn, but today many colleges and universities offer virtual classes, and many of these institutions offer virtual degrees.[10] Even venerable Harvard University has a small campus in the virtual world. Similarly, the business world has begun to embrace video conferencing and training webinars. And this is only the beginning. The church is sure to follow.

For the remainder of the book, I'm going to be careful when I use terms such as *internet* or *worldwide web* because they can obscure the digital revolution that is at hand. Instead, I will speak more in terms of the virtual worlds that are opening up around us — virtual worlds that soon will make the internet of today seem incredibly limited. The future of the internet lies not in its being a tool for emailing others but in its being an immersive world where many people will spend as much time as they do in the real world.[11] In the next few decades, the virtual world will equal or surpass the real world in its reach into and positioning in many aspects of our lives. For many people, the virtual world will be the world where they carry on more interactions and conduct more transactions than in the real world. It will be the place where they find love, soothe their feelings, make deals, and worship.

Some may dismiss this as hype or science fiction. After all, didn't socio-technological gurus in the early twentieth century predict that we'd have flying cars and moonbases before the year 2000? They did, and so we can agree that predicting the future is a shaky business. Nevertheless, many of the developments we will speak of are happening already, even if in a limited way. The evidence is strong that they will continue to happen in the next three decades. Of the one billion people online, an estimated seventy million are already regular participants in virtual worlds,[12] and that number continues to grow dramatically.[13] Virtual worlds are generating an estimated four billion dollars in annual revenue. And the sobering statistic: while no one knows exactly how much time residents spend in virtual worlds, a large percentage spend twenty or more hours *per week*, and many spend much, much more.[14]

At Secondlife.com, we get a good glimpse of what is on the horizon. Part of the second wave of the virtual evolution, Second Life has been growing exponentially since its inception in 2003. It boasts fourteen million members already. Second Life is not a website per se; it's a virtual world where an individual creates an avatar, becomes a resident, and tools around town accomplishing many of the same things a person in the real world is able to accomplish. There's more. As of 2007, Second Life residents exchange more than one and a half million dollars in commerce *every day* in that virtual world. Second Life even has its own currency (the Linden dollar), a real-estate market, virtual millionaires and crime rings, and virtual churches.

A Brave New Worship World

Today a new community for the people of God has begun. The church is evolving from the real world into the virtual world. At this point, most churches have merely stuck their little toes into the waters of the virtual world; they have a website with limited interaction, little more than a rudimentary, first-wave billboard. Some have caught the second wave and are a bit more advanced, offering a degree of interaction or spiritual instruction through blogs, downloadable teaching points, or sermon podcasts. And a number of churches have prepared for future waves by creating worship experiences in the virtual world.

One such church is LifeChurch.tv, based in Edmond, Oklahoma. Led by Senior Pastor Craig Groeschel, Innovation Pastor Bobby Gruenewald, and Internet Campus Pastor Brandon Donaldson, LifeChurch.tv offers several weekly worship experiences in their virtual church. Some of LifeChurch.tv's worship experiences use an internet-campus model — broadcasting services with text interaction — but LifeChurch.tv also has created the beginnings of a much more immersive virtual church in Second Life. LifeChurch.tv bought real estate, hired a developer, built a church building, and created seating for avatars to attend church each week. During its best weekend in 2007, LifeChurch.tv's internet campus (broadcast, plus

Because virtual worlds are in their infancy, there is no simple definition for them, and there is a great deal of confusion about worlds in general. Most researchers characterize a virtual world as some form of computer-mediated communication (which includes not only some parts of the internet but also any other digital network or electronic interface). A virtual world is in many ways more like virtual reality than email or blogging in that virtual worlds must have two basic elements: indwelt created space and social interaction.[a] Misunderstanding enters the picture when people try to describe a virtual world using words such as *real* or *imaginary*. This is the reason Edward Castronova, a virtual-world pioneer, suggests we refer to virtual worlds as "synthetic worlds" to avoid the assumption that they are fake or not real.[b] Virtual worlds are real, but they're created by people instead of by God.

One way to come to terms with the idea of the virtual world is to contrast it with other worlds. A quick tour of conceptual worlds reveals that there are many possible worlds, though we'll touch on only a few here. First, there is the *real world*. The real world is you, now, reading this book. From a biblical perspective, most or all other worlds are subsets of the real world, but they relate to the real world in very different ways. A *virtual world* is a created space where people can interact as if in the real world, but through some type of technological medium. Perhaps the best example of virtual worlds today are internet-based milieus such as

Second Life, World of Warcraft, or Lineage. Even though virtual worlds differ in several significant ways from the real world, virtual worlds, in their essence and nature, are just as real as the real world.[c]

In contrast to these two types of worlds are several others. A *fictional world* is a world created in the mind of a reader while reading a book, watching a movie, or engaging in any type of imaginative activity. If you read Tolkien or Lewis or watch *Tron* or *X-Men* and construct in your mind the events these works depict, you have laid the groundwork for a fictional world.[d] A fictional world is not the same as a virtual world because a fictional world is a mode of possibility and a virtual world is a mode of reality. An *imaginary world* is any type of world that is disconnected from the real world. Examples include daydreams or mythic places such as Asgard or the astral plane. A virtual world can be an imaginary world (as in the case of EverQuest or City of Heroes), but it doesn't have to be; a virtual world that obeys the laws of physics, doesn't allow animal avatars, and so on, doesn't qualify as an imaginary world. Let me say it again: virtual worlds can be imaginary, but they don't have to be; equating a virtual world with an imaginary world leads to inaccurate conclusions about faith and church in virtual worlds. Finally, an *augmented world* is a type of real world enhanced through technology.[e] A great example of this is the use of omnipresent and communicative Radio Frequency Identification devices, hologram technology, or cybernetics. A virtual world differs from an augmented world in that a virtual world occurs in a created space, whereas an augmented world originates in the real world.

Let's recap. We live in the real world. We can enter a virtual world through a digital interface, indwelling a synthetic space and interacting with other folks from the real world. A virtual world is not an augmented form of the real world, it's not typically a fictional world, and it can be but is not necessarily an imaginary world. Most important for our discussion, a virtual world is more likely than not to be a type of real world in synthetic space.

---

a. One of the better definitions: virtual worlds are "digitally constructed environments where peer-to-peer interaction can take place." See Maria Beatrice Bittarello, "Another Time, Another Space: Virtual Worlds, Myths and Imagination," *Online-Heidelberg Journal of Religions on the Internet* 3:1 (2008): 246.

b. Edward Castronova, *Synthetic Worlds: The Business and Culture of Online Games* (Chicago: University of Chicago Press, 2006).

c. It is beyond the scope of this book to defend this statement. Suffice it to say that reality doesn't have much to do with how a person perceives the world; it has more to do with the essence or nature of the world itself. Even though what we perceive in a virtual world may not seem real at times, that doesn't actually say anything about the essence of the thing we perceive. While there are several critiques of the reality of virtual worlds, there are many more significant proofs. Of course, much depends on how one defines the words *real* and *world*. Again, such a conversation is very important but is beyond the scope of this book because of its technical nature.

d. I have written elsewhere on the nature of worlds, especially the contrast between fictional worlds and real worlds. See Douglas Estes, *The Temporal Mechanics of the Fourth Gospel: A Theory of Hermeneutical Relativity in the Gospel of John*, Biblical Interpretation Series 92 (Leiden: Brill, 2008), 230–34.

e. Augmented worlds will play a major role in the evolution of the church in the twenty-first century, but they are not central to our topic. As an example, as hologram technology improves, it will redefine the multisite church by allowing a pastor to be hologrammatically telepresent at several different real-world worship venues at the same time.

Second Life) boasted an attendance of more than fourteen hundred people.[15] What is more, their internet campus launched its first real-world missions trip in 2007. People who had met only in the virtual world joined to build up the kingdom of God in the real world.

LifeChurch.tv is by no means alone. Believe it or not, the first virtual church was created way back in 1985, even before the advent of the web; an unnamed pioneering group of believers worshiped together through text-only interface. Since that time, other pioneers have slowly planted more churches amid the rapid changes to virtual-world interfaces. By some estimates, there were approximately thirty virtual churches by the year 2000.[16] Most of these early virtual churches were planted by tech-savvy individuals with little or no support. All of that changed in 2004. With the backing of the Methodist Church (UK), an experimental 3D virtual church called Church of Fools was launched. Because Church of Fools was an experiment, it functioned for only four months, but on its peak day, forty-one thousand people logged on for worship services.[17] Today there are already a couple of confirmed virtual megachurches, and there are more if you count hybrid streamers. There are virtual weddings, virtual Communion services, virtual baptisms, and virtual small groups doing real-world missions trips. From the Church of England's i-church to St. Hilda's Christian Goth Church (Second Life) to the Anglican Cathedral in Second Life (with seven worship services a week and growing) to the hundreds of other virtual churches, the church is beginning to be salt and light in our virtual worlds.[18]

The Post-Church Church

Skeptics may wonder why a person would choose to attend a virtual church, or even whether this issue matters. They may feel that virtual churches are the same as radio sermons and television ministries — a part of the modern church but not really all that different. They would be wrong. In contrast to radio and TV ministries, virtual churches

One of many virtual churches in the virtual world.

are products of two inexhaustible torrents redirecting twenty-first-century human development: the exponential rate of technological growth, and postmodernism. The confluence of these two great streams is creating a fertile floodplane for virtual churches to grow in. These churches will not be shadows of real-world churches, recorded and podcast, but something entirely new.

The role of radio and television in the ministry of the church developed in the modern era. Radio and TV are avenues for communication, but at their core they are unintelligent broadcasters: their greatest strength lies in their use of simple unidirectional monologs. As products of the modern era, they produced great wattage for churches and ministries, but a modern person would never confuse the church with a TV program or radio show. A modern person living in the modern world might watch their favorite pastor on TV or listen to him on the radio, perhaps even doing so more often than attending a bricks and mortar church, but they would never confuse those "ministries" with a church. They would never feel that the 2D pastor on their noise box was *their* pastor. As a whole, they would never feel that church membership means a commitment to listening to a radio sermon.[19]

However, as postmodernism increasingly becomes the world's default viewpoint, the concept of the church stretches and its borders become less pronounced. While postmodernism does *not* mean that "everything's relative," it does mean that binary reasoning (either/or, if/then, 0/1) is not the foundation for decision-making. As far as postmodern culture is concerned, a person is not limited to a choice between, for example, being either a Christian or a Buddhist; he or she can be either, neither, both, or a heterogeneous or homogeneous mixture of these two spiritualities. The same person can be a member of a real-world church, or a virtual-world church, or both, or neither, or somewhere in between. This may appear illogical to some modern readers, but I assure you, it is not.[20]

The virtual world is rapidly becoming more 3D, or immersive. Whereas radio and TV typically are monologs, virtual-world experiences are interactive and immersive. Instead of simply being broadcast to or monologed at, denizens of the virtual world are creating conversations and "hive minds" that produce truly collaborative experiences. For a growing number of people, especially individuals in the Millennial generation and beyond, virtual-world interactions can be far more authentic and far less awkward than real-world relationships, and for many younger people, interacting in the virtual world is the preferred method for social networking.[21] As the virtual world becomes more and more actualized in the coming decade, more and more people will turn to it for everyday interactions, including the fulfillment of their spiritual needs.

Let me be clear: I am *not* saying that in the near future, real-world churches will cease to exist and all things spiritual will come only from the virtual world. This will never happen. What will happen is that segments of society will be members not just of a real-world church but also of a virtual church. Many individuals, such as those who come from either tech-oriented or nonmainstream backgrounds, will prefer to worship in the virtual world because of the flexibility, transparency, diversity, and other innate strengths found in most virtual churches. They will first seek out spiritual experiences and conversations in the virtual world, for reasons we will discuss in the following chapters. The real-world church will change too, as the virtual-world continues to affect it.

Our Virtual Horizon

Today a new community of the people of God has begun, a community on the edge of the virtual world. Just as followers of God in the first century AD left their synagogues for house churches in search of more fulfilling faith communities, so too are ensuing generations poised to leave real-world churches for virtual-world churches. Just as the Christian diaspora from synagogue to church created a critical need for a theology of the church, so too does the emergence of virtual churches create the need for a theology of virtual church. Such an important task must not be left to the pragmatic and erratic currents of the virtual world.

In this book, we will explore many theological issues that relate to the church in the virtual world. Let me be clear at the outset: I will raise questions more than provide answers. This is the beginning of the conversation, not the recap. As Mark Brown, priest in charge of the Anglican Cathedral in Second Life, admitted to me, his church has only about 3 percent of it figured out; 97 percent is continual trial and error. "We don't have the answers," Mark said. "We don't have a manual." When you consider all of the long-standing debates over the nature and practices of the church, and then factor in the differences among North American and European and Asian traditions of the church — all of which enter the discussion — hammering out a theology of virtual church seems an almost impossible task. So to keep the discussion manageable, we'll engage in three spheres of inquiry — theological, missional, and ethical — and I have selected several issues that I believe are of paramount importance for virtual churches. In the theological sphere, we will discuss the nature, purpose, possibilities, and limitations of virtual churches. As much as possible, I will try to take into account different faith traditions, but mostly I will offer general insight and raise general questions. In the missional sphere, we will focus on the role of avatars, on virtual spirituality and ministry, and on the development of community in a virtual church. Finally, in the ethical sphere, we will take up concerns such as the question of virtual identity, personal holiness, and the dangers and limitations of niche ministries.

A final thought before we move on. The Christian church is engaging far less than 1 percent of the seventy million people who are active in the virtual world. This means the virtual world is by far the largest unreached people group on planet Earth. Simon Jenkins, one of the founders of Church of Fools, remarks that "it's like someone has created a new town and no one has thought to build a church there. It's almost scandalous."[22] We have great work to do.

chapter 2

The Cyber-Driven Church

One great thing about time off from work as a pastor is that you get to visit other people's churches.

During my brief writing sabbatical, I made plans to attend a church that was high on my list of churches to visit. After tracking down directions, service times, and the like, I worked it into my busy schedule.

That Sunday morning, as I walked to the church, I was a bit unsure how the visit would play out. The church belongs to a different denomination than mine and is in a part of the world I had never been to before, but even more than that, I just didn't know what the experience would be like. You know what it's like to go to a new church — big fear of the unknown.

As I walked down the street, I didn't see the church at first, even though I now know it to be quite large and distinct. The building was modeled after a glorious European cathedral, though sized down a bit. Surprisingly, the grey stone walls didn't make the building feel cold or unwelcoming.

As I got ready to enter the front door, I saw the pastor just inside and heard him greeting folks as they arrived. Oops, not ready for that yet, so I quickly backed out the door and read some information the church had posted out front. One of the information boards listed some of the church's beliefs and purposes, which set me much more at ease.

I tooled around outside until the pastor left the greeting area and got ready to start the service. I finally went into the building; its atmosphere was welcoming and I had only once or twice before been in services in a cathedral-like setting, and those services had been more performances than worship. I decided not to investigate the building any further because the worship service was starting.

Pews. Well, I hadn't done that in a while, so I found one near the back, of course. I realized after I had plopped down that I was awkwardly close to a young woman, and slightly embarrassed, I got up and shuffled down the pew a few more feet. Some other guy sat down next to me. The service began. The worship was way more liturgical than I was used to, but okay. The message by the pastor was way better than I had expected, though it was too brief, at least compared with what I was used to. It was orthodox, biblical, and meaningful. At the end of the service, one of the church's staff released a flight of doves that flew over the pews and out the open windows and doors in the front. Definitely had never seen that one before.

After the benediction, I said hi to a few people, and I saw the pastor make his way out the front of the building to greet everyone as they left. When I made it outside, I found that some of the attendees had stuck around and were joking about the accents of people from different parts of the world. I joined in the conversation for about ten minutes, but realizing time was passing, I said my goodbyes and headed back out the front yard and down the road.

Such was my first visit to the Anglican Cathedral, a virtual church in Second Life.

●

When it comes to talking about virtual churches, there is a really big elephant in the room:

 Is a virtual church a real, authentic, and valid expression of the church of Jesus Christ?

When I visited the Anglican Cathedral in Second Life, I was very surprised at just how real it seemed. It was my first time ever at a virtual church. I felt some apprehension as I approached. I walked around, read the info boards, and gathered brochures. I skirted by the pastor to avoid chatting, just to find my own place. I greeted my neighbors. I saw, heard, and experienced valid Christian worship. I fellowshiped with people after the service. I did everything I would have done had I visited most any other Protestant church service. The only difference was that the church — and I — was in the virtual world.

But was it real? Yes, as experiences go, it was a real experience. A few people may try to argue that the virtual world is not real,[1] but I was there, they weren't, and I'm telling you it was real in my experience, as well as in its demonstrable effects on real-world people and things. Many other people testify to the reality of virtual churches.[2] In fact, I would challenge any Christian who says that virtual churches are not real to go to a temple of a non-Christian god in Second Life and bow down and worship an idol. No sane Christian would take me up on this because they would quickly realize it is just "too real." We won't debate this issue any-more here. (We'll pick it up briefly in the next chapter.) What we will do is carefully consider whether a virtual church can be an authen-tic or genuine expression of a true Christian church. The litmus test for a church is much more stringent than for a program or minis-try. We need to do this in light of not just present-day, second-wave virtual-church experiences but also near-future-and-beyond virtual-church experiences. We will deal with this question directly in the next chapter or two, and then indirectly throughout the remainder of the book.

A bit of a warning: the level of debate over the nature of the church is so acute that the next few pages are a bit dense. Just dig in, hold on, and it will all be over soon, and then it's on to more enjoyable discussions.

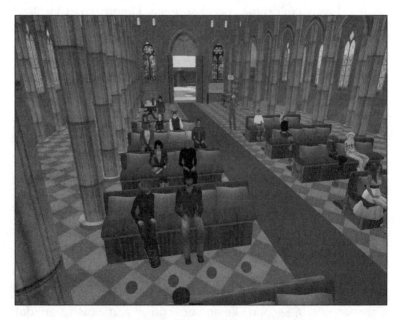

Anglican Cathedral in Second Life during a weekly
Sunday evening worship service.

A Church Virtual and True

Trying to determine the authenticity of virtual churches is tantamount to climbing a glacier — it seems foolhardy to observers and is terribly difficult for the climber. Quite a few obstructions stand in the way. First is the question of the nature of the virtual world itself. If the virtual world is an aspect or extension of the real world, as I believe,[3] and if this idea is both rational and defendable, then we may argue logically that it is possible for an authentic church to exist in the virtual world. Second, there is the problem of the nature of the church. Ecclesiology, or what we believe about the church, is a rather treacherous area of theology.[4] This is especially true for those (such as myself) who belong to evangelical or left-wing Protestant traditions that prefer to *do* church rather than *discuss* church.[5]

Another reason ecclesiology is a treacherous area is the personal nature of church; we all approach discussions of the church with presuppositions and opinions that come from our childhoods, family backgrounds, or other meaningful, but not necessarily standardized, experiences.[6] I think back to my grandfather, a lay leader in his church, who passed away when I was a boy. If he were here today, he would hardly recognize the church I pastor as being a real church. He would struggle with our form of the church. Likewise, my initial experiences in African tribal churches led me to the same problem — until I was able to grasp the huge cultural shift. Hans Küng says it best: "Our concept of the Church is basically influenced by the form of the Church at any given time."[7] It will be tempting for many moderns (and those foreign to the culture of the virtual world) to reject the authenticity of virtual churches simply because they are not forms of church that they are accustomed to.

Let's survey the landscape.[8] There are a few neo-Luddites who grudgingly accept the inevitability of virtual worlds but despise the idea of virtual churches.[9] A large number of writers and thinkers understand the power of the virtual world for the kingdom but do not believe virtual churches are authentic churches in their own right.[10] Some of these folks suggest virtual churches could be good parachurch ministries.[11] There are also a good number of scholars and theorists who, for a variety of reasons, don't fully accept virtual churches as genuine but don't necessarily deny their validity either.[12] And then there are those who earnestly believe that a virtual church can be an authentic church of God.[13] Let's find out.

Church Refined

The English word *church* comes from an early Germanic expression (derived from the Greek) meaning "the Lord's." It was most likely a reference to the building used by Christians for worship and, all things considered, is not a very good translation of the primary New Testament word for the people of God, *ekklesia*.[14] In today's English, we would probably translate *ekklesia* as "assembly" or "town-hall meeting" rather than "church" (though we could still use *church* for the building). You may have heard that the etymological root of *ekklesia* means "called-out ones," but this is not really true; it's an exegetical fallacy.[15] An *ekklesia* is simply a gathering, an assembly, or a town-hall meeting of citizens, and in the New Testament sense of the word, it refers to citizens of the kingdom of God.

Beyond the use of this simple descriptor for the church, the Bible never defines or delimits the concept of an *ekklesia*. Instead, the Bible speaks of the church using a large variety of metaphors, such as "the body of Christ" or "community of the Holy Spirit."[16] The result is that it's impossible for us to privilege one concept of the church to the exclusion of others.[17] This variety of metaphors leads to many disagreements over the parameters of a church. In fact, it's quite ironic that the biblical idea of church is not concrete but is very much a "metaphorical construct," an expression that we can use to describe virtual worlds.[18]

One of the historic, long-standing debates about the nature of the church is whether the universal or the local idea of the church is the most important for discussions about the church. Conventional wisdom holds that if you want to prove that a group is a church, make your case from the standpoint of the universal church, since the universal church is a more nebulous image than the local church. The problem with this approach is that about 85 percent of the uses of *ekklesia* in the New Testament are oriented toward the local church. As John Hammett explains, "The focus in New Testament usage is on local churches."[19] We could argue that the proportion of local to universal church usage is skewed in the New Testament, since almost all of the occurrences of the *ekklesia* concept are in occasional letters to local churches, but we won't. The local church is what matters in this discussion, because that is the paradigm most virtual churches will follow. Local churches in a virtual world.[20]

Before we go farther, some may wonder, What *is* a virtual church? It is critical that we do not confuse a virtual church with, say, a website of a real-world church. A virtual church is not a website (building or place), a podcast (ritualized institution), or a blog (fellowship or activity). A virtual church is a place where people professing to have faith in Jesus Christ gather regularly to be in meaningful community appointed to build up the kingdom — or more specifically, a virtual church *is* the confessing people gathering in a synthetic world. At this point, let's agree on two working definitions that will carry us through the rest of this book. First, let's loosely define a church as a *localized assembly of the people of God dwelling in meaningful community with the task of building the kingdom.* In a way, it is perhaps more important that we agree on what a church is not: a church is not a building or place, a ritualized institution, or a fellowship or activity. Second, let's loosely define a virtual church as a *virtually localized assembly of the people of God dwelling in meaningful community with the task of building the kingdom.*

AREN'T VIRTUAL CHURCHES JUST SUPPLEMENTS TO REAL-WORLD CHURCHES?

One common assumption made by people unfamiliar with virtual churches is that virtual churches are simply supplements to real-world churches, that they function like small groups do, offering more opportunities for spiritual growth beyond the Sunday-morning worship service. For example, in a recent book about online religion, Heidi Campbell constantly reassures her readers that, at least at the time of her research, most virtual churchgoers see virtual churches as supplements to churches in the real world rather than as distinct churches.[a] Why not leave it at that, make everyone happy, and call it a day?

First, because it's a losing proposition. Of all the virtual churches I am familiar with, none consider their church a supplement in any way. It may be that this is a good thing. After all, if the virtual world, filled with tens of millions of people, is real, shouldn't it have a real church? As an analogy, developers in Dubai are creating synthetic islands on which they hope to sell residential and resort properties. Isn't it important that Christians want to be able to put a church on those synthetic islands — not just a supplement or a small group but a real church? It is. So too in the virtual world. It's possible that if a synthetic world cannot contain a real church, that world is unreachable; the cause of Christ is lost in that world. In that instance, the kingdom loses, and virtual churches lose. Not only that, but real-world churches lose too. Think of it like this: if a young pastor plants a church of a different but orthodox Christian denomination in the shadow of my real-world church, it would be easy to get jealous and talk down his church. (Shamefully, this happens all the time in our world.) But really, we're on the same team. One virtual-church pastor confided to me, off the record, that at a recent large pastors' conference, the number-one comment made to him — also off the record — about why "they" (other pastors) were opposed to virtual churches is that "they" were afraid virtual churches would steal "their" people. But quite the opposite is the case; many virtual churches reach people with the gospel who would never go to a real-world church but over time might become interested in getting involved in a safe real-world church. Could this be the Starbucks phenomenon? Conventional wisdom holds that if Starbucks moves into a neighborhood, it will kill the mom-and-pop coffeehouses, but studies demonstrate that the opposite happens. Mom-and-pops actually grow because of Starbucks.[b] Could it be that virtual churches benefit all churches? It is in the interest of every real-world pastor to get over our insecurity and allow God to be who we claim he is, not just to see more real-world churches planted but to see more virtual churches planted as well. More good churches is always a good thing!

Second, because it's the wrong question. Implied in the question is that we in the church should be safe; we should play nice and not push boundaries. I think most of us agree where that will get us. The church must push boundaries in every age and every generation for the cause of Christ. This requires us to move away from either/or thinking into both/and thinking — it's not either a real-world church or a virtual-world church; it's both real-world churches and virtual-world churches, everyone working together for the kingdom. Labeling virtual churches as supplements is like giving them the award for honorable mention or a gold star for perfect attendance. It's nice, but not the support or constructive criticism they need. One thing virtual churches could use is good, healthy, constructive dialog with real-world churches — and not being looked down upon the way just about every new group of churches has been looked down upon throughout church history by more traditional forms of the church.

---

a. Heidi Campbell, *Exploring Religious Community Online: We Are One in the Network*, Digital Formations 24 (New York: Peter Lang, 2005), 161, 191. Anecdotally, I have not found this to be the case, especially with marginal virtual-church attendees.
b. Taylor Clark, "Don't Fear Starbucks: Why the Franchise Actually Helps Mom and Pop Coffeehouses," *Slate*, December 28, 2007.

To qualify a virtual church as an authentic church, we need to investigate virtual churches in light of biblical images. The limited scope of this book prevents us from examining every passage pertaining to the church, but we will consider three important biblical thought-patterns: (1) Christian community in the Gospels, (2) the early Jerusalem church in Acts, and (3) the church in New Testament letters to individual churches in Asia Minor. It's also important to remember that we don't have to scrutinize every statement in the Bible on the church because almost all of the discussions on the church are spiritual — life, heart, soul issues — rather than about physical parameters that contrast or distinguish virtual-world and real-world churches.

An obvious starting point for our discussion is Jesus' popular statement about his involvement with his gathered followers: "For where two or three come together in my name, there am I with them" (Matt. 18:20). This statement concludes Jesus' explanation of accountability in the Christian community and is not a declaration about the nature of the church per se.[21] Still, we must note two important principles. First, the church is not just a gathering of disciples but a gathering of disciples under the authority of Jesus (Eph. 4:15, 23 – 24). If my wife and I take a family from church to the mall for lunch, we are not the church. Yes, we are still a part of the universal church, but we are not a local body of believers as envisioned throughout the New Testament. Only if we agree to become a local church and uphold biblical precedence for a local church and submit the authority of the group to the headship of Christ can we call ourselves a church. Second, and more important, this passage in Matthew establishes the critical necessity for a church to be a church: a church cannot be the church without the presence of God (Eph. 2:22). No Jesus, no church. No Spirit, no church. The allusion to which Jesus refers when he makes this statement is that he, as the divine

Son, must be present in the full glory of the Godhead when a church gathers for us to consider it to be an authentic church.[22] Therefore, if a virtual church claims to be a church, it cannot simply be a group of Christians in voluntary association, whether in the real world or the virtual world. They must gather together for Christ, with Christ present.

One story in the Gospels that is not regularly part of discussions about the church but is particularly important for our study is John 4. This story relates Jesus' discussion with an unnamed Samaritan woman at a well while he was in Samaria. Since legalistic Jews of the day looked down on Samaritan women as unclean, the Samaritan woman is at first skeptical of Jesus' claims but slowly begins to believe (John 4:9, 39). After she concedes that Jesus may be a prophet (4:19), she says something a bit unusual and out of context: "Our fathers [meaning the Samaritans] worshiped on this mountain, but you Jews [like Jesus] claim that the place where we must worship is in Jerusalem." It's hard to say whether the Samaritan woman asked forthrightly,[23] or asked just to create a diversion.[24] The Samaritan woman probably expected Jesus to launch into some unfavorable exposition of the minutiae of Jewish law — she was used to Jews boasting about possessing a special place for worship.[25] Instead, Jesus tells her "a time is coming when you will worship the Father neither on this mountain nor in Jerusalem … a time is coming and has now come when the true worshipers will worship the Father in spirit and truth, for they are the kind of worshipers the Father seeks" (4:21 – 23).

Jesus' unexpected response reveals several things. First, true worship of God will never again be tied to a specific, geographic locale.[26] The Samaritan woman had accepted for herself an inferior status because of a mistaken understanding of the nature of worship. Jesus corrects her using the double negation "neither on this mountain nor in Jerusalem" — he eliminates geography from the question of true worship. Second, Jesus' response in the original language is general in whom it refers to and specific in what believers are to do.[27] Jesus' point to the Samaritan woman is unmistakable: true worship hinges not on geography (and by extrapolation religious codes) but on the Spirit's presence in the midst of worshipers (Matt. 18:20).

Some may argue that John 4 is concerned not with the church per se but with Christian worship in general, but such a claim depends on a false dichotomy, since the New Testament doesn't prescribe individualistic worship as is common in the Western mindset. The best way to read Jesus' statement is to take it at face value: true worshipers of God worship together by the Spirit, not by geographic location.[28] Since we have already discounted declarations of worship by individuals, John 4 is a powerful argument for the viability and validity of virtual churches. A true biblical church is not limited to or defined by location, except for one: being in the Spirit.

Acts 2:42–47 records a familiar description of the church in Jerusalem after Pentecost; it describes a unique situation in the history of the early church marked by radical unselfishness and togetherness. Many people mistakenly try to make this into a complete paradigm for modern churches without taking into account its historical and specific nature.[29] This claim doesn't work because it doesn't take the context of the whole passage into account; advocates of an out-of-context reading of Acts 2 can't claim that a modern church must operate in this type of radical communality unless they also mandate that a modern church must worship at the temple in Jerusalem or possess apostles who perform signs and wonders (as in Acts 2:45).[30] We won't solve all of the problems with the common mishandling or idealization of Acts 2 here, but we will argue one point: the everyday *koinonia*, or intimate community, referred to in Acts 2 is possible and even commonplace in virtual churches (based on the testimony of members of virtual churches).[31] While it is possible to prove that virtual churches can possess *koinonia*, is it the same degree of *koinonia* as real-world churches? We'll examine this question in later chapters. Many readers will wonder how virtual churches can share a common meal together, especially Communion; we'll take up that issue in chapter 5. For now, we can say that the virtual world does not prevent us from intimate community and from loving and demonstrating unselfishness toward other believers (united in a church) in an Acts 2 way. As we will discover, there are trade-offs; some aspects of the virtual world probably discourage some types of community experiences, whereas some aspects of the virtual world actually encourage other types of community experiences.

The final biblical examples we'll look at come from a couple of assertions about the church that are in the New Testament letters. Most of the more significant metaphors such as "the body of Christ" or "the people of God" are compatible with a virtual church. In his book *Images of the Church in the New Testament*, Paul Minear compiles a list of ninety-six different biblical metaphors for the church, none of which contradict or deny the authenticity of a virtual church. Most of these metaphors build on what we have talked about — believers gathered under the headship of Christ. A few are architectural or construction metaphors (for example, 1 Cor. 3:10 – 11 and Eph. 2:19 – 22), but each image is a metaphor for what God does through the Spirit, never for a physical building (1 Peter 2:4 – 5).[32]

Andrew Careaga, author of *eMinistry*, tells the story of one online discussion in which a moderator cited Hebrews 10:25 ("Let us not give up meeting together, as some are in the habit of doing, but let us encourage one another — and all the more as you see the Day approaching") as an argument against virtual churches.[33] In the original language of the New Testament, this verse uses unusual, somewhat apocalyptic language to contextualize the gathering of the church. The verse implies that while some Jewish folks may have been tempted to return to the legalistic Judaism of their day, committed believers were to continue gathering, looking toward the return of Jesus. The verse is more about staying united, not falling away, and awaiting God's plan than it is about modern church meetings. Either way, this verse doesn't invalidate virtual churches; if anything, it encourages a regular united time of worship and community that is possible in both the real and virtual worlds. As we'll discuss in later chapters, Hebrews 10:25 as popularly understood could be equally or in some situations even *more* true of the average virtual church than the average real-world church, especially if we consider that a virtual church has far fewer limitations on how often or how long it can meet. Anecdotal evidence suggests that virtual churchgoers are on average more participatory than what we may expect in a typical real-world church. For example, Anglican Cathedral in Second Life and i-church both base their ministry schedules more on regular involvement than weekly attendance. This is a biblical call for staying united as a localized people of God.[34]

Finally, two similar statements by Paul require our attention. To the church in Colossae, Paul writes, "For though I am absent from you in body, I am present with you in spirit and delight to see how orderly you are and how firm your faith in Christ is" (Col. 2:5). And to the church in Corinth, Paul writes, "Even though I am not physically present, I am with you in spirit. And I have already passed judgment on the one who did this, just as if I were present. When you are assembled in the name of our Lord Jesus and I am with you in spirit, and the power of our Lord Jesus is present, hand this man over to Satan, so that the sinful nature may be destroyed and his spirit saved on the day of the Lord" (1 Cor. 5:3 – 5). We need to be careful to handle these difficult texts correctly, not to make them say more or less than they say. Here's what we know: Paul is writing to two local churches from which he is physically absent but with which he is still united through the power of the Holy Spirit.[35] When Paul says he is absent in body but present in spirit, he does not mean this in a metaphysical, New Age, mind over matter sort of way. He just means he is united with them. Even though Paul is not physically present, he still engages with both of these local churches in not only worship practices but also church discipline. It is fair to say that Paul believes himself to be a part of these local churches, even though he may not be geographically close.[36] It is also interesting to note that Paul doesn't say this just one time but makes this clear two times in two different churches and regarding two different situations. The bottom line is this: Paul does not appear to view geography or space as a factor that can limit his participation in the church.[37]

The problem with our investigation of biblical texts to determine the validity of virtual churches is that the Bible just doesn't define the church in spatial or geographical terms. Minear summarizes it best: "For many moderns who crave an exact calculation of the boundaries of the church this is a distressing feature of the New Testament … that the church is a divine mystery that cannot be circumscribed by doctrinal or institutional measurement."[38] Much to the chagrin of neo-Luddites, excluding virtual churches on purely biblical grounds is an almost impossible task. What about on the grounds of theology and tradition?

From Traditional to Virtual

Whether we like it or not (or are willing to admit it or not), most of what we believe about the church (after our presuppositions) comes from church tradition. During my writing sabbatical, I had lunch with a good friend of mine who teaches theology at a major denominational seminary in the US. Over orange chicken and fortune cookies, I asked him to play devil's advocate with me, to argue against the validity of virtual churches. What was interesting about our mock debate was that my friend kept coming back to church tradition and doctrine, rather than Scripture, to attack the idea of virtual church (contrary to what I had anticipated). The problem, of course, is this: the value you place on church tradition for modern discussions may be tremendously different from the value I place on it. We may even be at odds. Our denominational contexts and church backgrounds really make a difference in this regard.

Being a Free Church pastor, I value church tradition only inasmuch as it allows me to better understand and interpret the Bible. Some of you will feel I have quite an impoverished view of the church! But I do care about the church in all of its historical forms, which is why discussing virtual churches as a valid type of local church must also be done in light of church history and tradition. Of course, there is no way I can make everyone happy, so as with the previous section, I have selected a few of the most important and reasonable formulations of the church. Most are from the early church or are representative of Protestant theology.

As with our investigation of the Bible, a considerable complication arises when we turn to church tradition to ascertain the authenticity of virtual churches. For most of the history of the church — some fifteen hundred years — pastors and theologians never developed systematic studies of the church that would allow us to argue parameters. Only the lead-up to the Protestant Reformation generated organized ecclesiologies.[39] Since the Reformation, the rapid splintering of Protestant Christianity plus the destruction of the medieval view of knowledge by modernity has created a multitude of narrowly focused views of the church. Nicholas Healy calls these narrow views "blueprint ecclesiologies," because they purport to serve as a blueprint or foundation for delineating church.[40] While this way of thinking also has affected non-Protestant theologians, it is so acute in Protestant groups that it would be impossible today to define a Protestant view of the church that many other people would agree with.[41] We can suggest that anyone who says the church must have such-and-such parameters based on the Bible or the teaching of the early church is almost always on shaky ground.

Can virtual churches bear the "marks of a church" in light of Christian history and theology?

One of the earliest discussions about the church occurs in the letters of Ignatius, the late-first-century bishop of Antioch. In his letter to the church in Smyrna, Ignatius defines the church in light of its intent and authority: "Where the overseer may appear, there let the people [of God] be; where Jesus Christ is, there is the whole church."[42] He views the church not as a physical organization but as a shepherded assembly. Polycarp, the early-second-century bishop of Smyrna, introduces his letter to the church in Philippi by reminding his readers that the church is "residing as an alien" in that city.[43] He uses an Old Testament metaphor to remind the church that it transcends this physical world.[44] Irenaeus, the late-second-century bishop of Lyons, depicted the church solely in terms of its union with the Holy Spirit.[45] Tertullian, the early-third-century theologian of Carthage, writes that "where three are, the church is, even if they are just lay people," echoing Ignatius and characterizing the church as a gathered community of regular folks within Trinitarian license (as implied by the number three, in contrast to Matt. 18:20).[46] Likewise Origen, a mid-third-century theologian from Alexandria, describes the church as the "gathering of all saints" and writes that it "is [made] from the sum of many believers."[47] In the late-third-century, Cyprian, the bishop of Carthage, defended the unity of the church, explaining that while the church will exist in different parts, all of the parts work together to make the true church of Christ.[48] In light of each of these descriptions of the church, a virtual church appears to be a viable church. In fact, the early church fathers chose to place a tremendous emphasis on the church as a place of good doctrine, true spirituality, and apostolic authority — not location or structures. To them the church was much more of a spiritual gathering than a physical meeting.[49]

A frequently used mark of the church throughout Christian history is the early creeds of the church. The so-called Apostles' Creed, which is claimed to date back to the apostles, classifies the church only as "holy," as the creed itself focuses mostly on Jesus.[50] Similarly, the so-called Nicene Creed portrays the church with four adjectives: one, holy, catholic, and apostolic. At first glance, none of these marks would seem to invalidate a virtual church; a virtual church could be united with other churches, sanctified in its people and spirit, catholic because it represents the whole of God's plan (though we will discuss this more later), and apostolic because its intent is to be sent into the world as Jesus and his disciples. Of course, the greatest difficulty with using these creeds to define a church is discerning what these four words really mean — theologians have been debating their sense for two thousand years without much agreement or success in finding common ground.[51] We'll leave that debate to them.

In the nearly one thousand years between the time of the early church fathers and the Reformation, the idea of the church evolved from spiritual community to physical empire. This idea probably originated with Augustine, the famous bishop of Hippo, who likened the church to the eternal city of God, which opposed the temporal city of the world.[52] Augustine also perceived the church to be a society of redemption and divine love.[53] Many of Augustine's ideas appear to be compatible with virtual churches, especially in regard to his philosophical-ascetic inclination. Later medieval churchmen picked up his church-as-empire motif and amplified it to create a highly institutionalized organization (as seen in the works of Peter Lombard and Thomas Aquinas). Because the ideas of the medieval church are out of vogue in almost all circles, we'll move on.

The Reformation was a sea change in the development of the idea of the church. Jan Hus, a protoreformer from Bohemia, opposed the rigid ecclesiastical structure of the Roman Catholic Church by promoting the idea that the church is a free assembly of believers.[54] Martin Luther, the German reformer, followed this idea and the early creeds in large part, seeing the church as a gathering of believers "who hear the voice of their Shepherd."[55] Luther didn't even like the word *church*, preferring instead *community* or *assembly*. Later in his life, he endorsed his followers' definition of the church as "the gathering of all believers, in which the gospel is purely preached and the holy sacraments are administered in accord with the gospel."[56] If we accept this classic Lutheran definition, a virtual church can succeed in the areas of community and the proclamation of the gospel but may run into obstacles with the sacraments or ordinances.[57] Luther's idea of the priesthood of all believers was a critical development in Protestant theology, and it led to the development of atypical church communities, including some that we find in the virtual world.

John Calvin, the Swiss reformer, built his ideas about church on the Augsburg Confession but contrasted with Luther and Hus on the structure of the visible church; he was keen on adding orderliness to the new Protestant churches. Perhaps it's understandable that he added a third mark to Luther's two: not just pure worship and properly administered sacraments but also correct church government and discipline.[58] These three marks of the church became popular in the confessions of early modern churches, and many churches still hold to them today. This third mark of correct church government and discipline is quite possible for virtual churches to bear, and we will discuss this in more detail in chapters 6 and 8.

In contrast with the past, debating the details of the nature of the church is one of the hallmarks of modern theology.[59] What this means is there's no way we can begin to cover all the recent formulations, so we'll just hit a few highlights. One recent theory of the church is church as *koinonia*, or communion, a popular position held primarily by Roman Catholic and Orthodox scholars.[60] Communion ecclesiology asserts that since God — Father, Son, and Spirit — dwells solely in divine communion, true faith, worship, and even human existence can occur only within the communion of a church. Since it's more of an idea than a prescription, communion ecclesiology appears to be compatible with some, if not most, virtual-church ideologies. Another modern theory of the church argues that the orientation of the church should be church as mission. Lesslie Newbigin, an Anglican missionary, argued that the church is missional in its very nature, not just in its duty. Since Newbigin's ideas are a critique of the Western church-as-empire, they fit very well with the dynamic spirit of virtual churches engaging a new world without any vestiges of Christendom.

We will cover just three more people's thoughts. Karl Barth, the famous twentieth-century theologian, advocated a view of the church that brings the heart of Reformed theology into the sense of the Free Church — the community of God led by the Word and the Spirit and sent into the world.[61] Barth's iconic definition of the church — "The church is *when* it takes place" (emphasis mine) — recognizes the power of God's people not limited by spatial and geographical boundaries.[62] Hans Küng cultivated a powerful vision in his magisterial work *The Church*, contending that the people of God form a real, tangible church that is at once broken and redeemed — a communion of pilgrims in a fallen world. Küng calls for the empowerment of everyone in the body of Christ to use the gifts (charisms) given by God. Given the collaborative nature of the virtual world, virtual churches may be able to fulfill Küng's dream for the church in ways that real-world churches never dreamed possible. Finally, my view of the church: the Free Church. As a participant in and practitioner of this ecclesiological tradition, I believe virtual churches have much to offer the kingdom. I point to one popular Free Church thinker: Rick Warren. His book *The Purpose-Driven Church* has had the greatest impact on the practice of the church at the turn of the millennium. Warren's biblical understanding of church is that it must have five marks, or purposes: evangelism, worship, discipleship, fellowship, and ministry. As we will see, virtual churches are quite capable of accomplishing each of these purposes.

Much like our survey of biblical evidence, there is little in church history that strongly supports or strongly refutes the idea of a virtual church. Clearly, though, there are many insights from church history that these newbie churches must consider as they build communities to reach the virtual world for the cause of Christ. Just as the church at large has made many mistakes and wrong turns over the course of its history, so too will virtual churches make many mistakes as they grow. The good news is that virtual churches can and should learn a great deal from real-world churches and their shared history.

The SimChurch

In the year 2000, Will Wright, a well-known computer-game designer, created a game about life. The Sims was revolutionary — you play a person doing mundane things that aren't as much fun in the real world as they are in the virtual world. Many people at the time (myself included) thought the game would flop, but instead, it's currently the bestselling computer game in history. Somehow, the shift from the real world to the virtual world transformed what we take for granted into something meaningful.

The church has been around the block for two thousand years, and our world takes it for granted. As we attempt to engage the post-Christian world with the truth of the gospel, we will need to draw up new blueprints for being the church; it is absolutely necessary that we don't allow church culture to hold us back from reformulating the church for this time and place.[63] Virtual churches recreate the taken-for-granted church and put it in front of those people who increasingly choose to inhabit the virtual world. We should not be surprised by this: the history of the Christian church is marked as much by innovation as by tradition, most of the innovation coming from pioneers who didn't have all the answers but just rolled up their sleeves and started. However we may feel about it, virtual churches are many, are growing, and are here to stay.

In this chapter, we briefly surveyed biblical and historical perspectives on the church and found little evidence to argue against the validity of virtual churches. Of course, the writers of the New Testament and the church fathers never envisioned this problem, but their trust in the power of God working through the church unlimited by time and space is significant. We may say it clearly: anyone who claims a virtual church is not a real, authentic church must do so outside of the Bible and without the support of the majority of church history. This is not to say that there are not serious questions facing virtual churches as they strive for legitimacy. We can help this situation by not polarizing this issue: it shouldn't be real-world churches versus virtual-world churches, or Baptist churches versus Presbyterian churches, but the different parts of the body of Christ extending grace to churches that may be a little different from each other but still uphold the same Lord, the same Spirit, the same gospel, and the same faith.

Whether in the real or the virtual world, "All individual communities receive one and the same Gospel, all receive the same mission and the same promise. All are subject to the grace of one and the same Father, have one and the same Lord, are inspired by one and the same Holy Spirit in their charisms and their ministries. They believe one and the same faith, are sanctified by one and the same baptism, and refreshed by one and the same meal."[64]

But — and it's a big but — the fact that a virtual-world church can be a real church doesn't mean that just *any* virtual group or virtual building calling itself a church is a real, authentic, biblical church. As in the real world, there is more to being a church than just the name. Just because someone creates a beautiful church building in Second Life and decides to offer services doesn't mean they've started a real church. We need to explore this a bit more deeply. Just what does it mean to *be* a church in the virtual world?

chapter 3

A Telepresent People of God

The most popular church of the twenty-first century may turn out to be a virtual church. On May 19, 2004, more than forty-one thousand people visited the Church of Fools, a virtual church based in the UK. In the US, in Korea, this would have caused a stir, but in Europe? It set off a media firestorm. Who ever would have thought that forty-one thousand people in Europe would be interested in church? News outlets from the *London Times* to the BBC to CNN covered the story.

Most of us are aware that the post-Christian spirit has hit Western Europe far harder than North America. Church attendance there averages around 10 percent of the population each Sunday.[1] I remember one of my first days as a graduate student in the UK; on my way to market, I passed several beautiful church buildings, with steeples and stained-glass windows, that had been converted into gothic nightclubs and trendy office complexes. Compared with other parts of the world, the church in Europe seemed to be on its deathbed.

So what caused forty-one thousand people to come together in the virtual world for church? Perhaps many of those people came because of media hype, out of curiosity, or even to cause trouble. But all forty-one thousand?

The creators of the Church of Fools experiment planned to host services for just three months. But the people who joined the church passionately petitioned its leaders to keep the church open longer. Many deemed this miniworld to be sacred space. Even though the Church of Fools leadership team was unable to continue worship services because of financial issues, they responded to regular attenders' wishes and left the "building" standing for private worship and reflection.

While the Church of Fools was making headlines on both sides of the Atlantic, something happened within the Church of Fools that made headlines among the group of its founders. The Church of Fools creators had designed the church primarily to reach out to people who were not Christians — to be evangelistic. And it did that. But they found something unexpected in their virtual creation: real community.[2] This community had blossomed and continued to grow.

People from around the world petitioned the creators of the now inactive Church of Fools to create another church. Soon, they did: St. Pixels. Even before St. Pixels became a church, it had more than fifteen hundred registered members. That's impressive in any world, real or virtual.

St. Pixels opened in 2008, and its community keeps growing. One of St. Pixels' sister websites has an area where people can anonymously review churches. When asked about St. Pixels, one mystery worshiper said the best thing about it is "probably the sense of community. It sounds odd, but this really works."[3]

●

It seems impossible that people scattered all over the world can sit in front of machines and somehow form real community. And it *is* impossible if we look at the computer to try to understand such an outlandish claim. The computer doesn't hold the answer; people do. It is the God-designed relational nature of humans that allows people from different backgrounds to meet and form a church, that allows people to aid their enemies or unite in family groups, and that allows people to use technology to create community. It's not the technology that creates community; it's the people.

Can virtual community really work? How can virtual churches reenergize Christian community?

Scientific and technological revolutions generally don't happen incrementally; they occur in waves.[4] The problem with waves is that they give you no time to adjust. One minute you're dry, the next you're immersed. The same is true with community in the virtual world. A large and rapidly growing segment of the world's population is immersed in virtual worlds. And it seems many traditional church leaders would rather stay high and dry because they don't see how participating in a virtual world counts as real community.

We expect a virtual church to have real, authentic fellowship and community in order to be a real, authentic local church. One of the most common questions one encounters whenever the subject of virtual churches comes up is whether a virtual church can be a true community, and it is the biggest objection to virtual churches that skeptics seem to make. Most skeptics I have come across claim that physical presence is required for people to be properly united as a church. After all, they ask, how can virtual churchgoers greet their fellow believers with a holy kiss (1 Peter 5:14) in a synthetic world?[5]

So is physical presence really necessary for real community? Or is it important, but not required? To answer this question we must look at the nature of community and talk about what it means to be present, as well as to be present in a community. Most of us make assumptions about the nature of presence and community according to our cultural background — though a quick survey of ancient and modern, urban and rural mores reveals clear distinctions between these two words. For us to swim into the coming technological and societal wave and minister to maturing digital generations, we'll need to be more than present; we'll need to be the telepresent people of God.

A MUSH of Fools

Early virtual worlds were MUDs (multi-user DUNGENs).[6] Depending on whom you ask, a MUD is a multi-user virtual space created for gaming or social interaction. The first MUDs were created in the late 1970s and were mostly a form of text-based adventure game for early computer researchers who were lucky enough to have access. Think of playing Zork on the internet. Over time, MUDs spawned a variety of virtual offspring and grand-offspring; a great example today is MMOGs (massively multiplayer online games) or MMORPGs (massively multiplayer online role-playing games) such as Everquest, World of Warcraft, or Lord of the Rings Online. These games each have tens of thousands of communities of millions of committed players. Another offspring is the MUSH (multi-user shared hallucination) — a multi-user space that is limited only by the imaginations of the users.

Is a virtual church just a MUSH, one big shared hallucination? I'm sure many skeptics consider *any* form of the church to be a MUSH. Christians like to testify that our beloved churches and our faith in God are not hallucinations but real. At the same time, many of these same Christians criticize virtual community as unreal. Yet what do we do with the growing chorus of Christians who testify to finding real community in virtual churches and internet campuses? Studies show not only that people *are* finding real community in virtual churches[7] but even that some testify that their synthetic churches have a *greater* sense of community than their real-world churches.[8]

And just what is the deal with virtual relationships? Why is it that many people will go to great lengths to avoid their neighbor in the supermarket, but those same people are more than willing to go up to a complete stranger online and strike up a conversation? Me, I'm an introvert. My favorite kind of restaurant is one in which the only people present are me and the waitstaff. But why is it that when I switch from myself in the real world to my avatar self in the virtual world I feel compelled to talk to the next avatar that appears near me? What makes community in the virtual world almost (dare I say it?) addictive?

The seemingly addictive nature of virtual community derives from two powerful forces at work in all people. First, it originates with the innate, God-given need and desire to relate to other people. It's Trinitarian; it's genetic. Even if we suppress this need, as everyone does at certain times for various reasons, we in the end still seek out relationships with others in some form or another to fulfill this need. Maybe it's better to say that in each of our lives there is a constant tension between our pulling inward and God's calling us outward. Or perhaps better to say that when there is a relational vacuum in our lives, someone or something will rush in to fill it. Second, the seemingly addictive nature of virtual community also stems from how we understand our sense of presence as people. We can start with the anonymous nature of virtual-world interaction, but it is actually much more than that. I can go to a city that I have never been to before, even dress and look differently than I normally do, and I will be anonymous, but it will not free me to start telling passersby my life story. (Far from it; I'll just go look for an empty restaurant.) At the same time, synthetic worlds free us to follow our *imago Dei* need for greater depths of relationship not only by creating a feeling of anonymity but also by stripping away the physical hang-ups and fears we have when we are "present" in the real world, and by generating opportunities for lots of "optional relationships" — relationships with people we never expect to relate to again that free us to be very, sometimes overly, intimate.[9] Optional relationships are more than anonymous relationships because they are not just secretive but also compartmentalized and insulated. It's not the anonymity or the electronic medium that causes this; it's the change in presence.

The Essence of Presence

If we want community to flourish in the virtual world, we'll need to scrutinize our learned understanding of presence. Most people raised and educated in the Western world think of presence or being present as a physical act; in grade school, we learned to answer "present" when the teacher took roll, because our bodies were there, even if our minds were outside running wild and free. We have been taught to think of ourselves as being present wherever our bodies are, even if our minds (or hearts or spirits) wander. Though defining presence simply as the location of our bodies is one of the foundational bricks of the modern Western understanding of the world, it is not a God-given or biblical idea.[10] Westerners' ideas about presence mostly trace back to René Descartes, one of the fathers of the modern Western worldview — the "I think, therefore I am" guy.[11] In his influential book *Meditations*, Descartes sets out the premise of what we refer to as mind-body dualism — the idea that a human being has two distinct parts: a body and a mind (or soul).[12]

Though his ideas on the split between body and mind had an incredible impact on the Western worldview, it is less well-known that Descartes, in his *Meditations*, also wondered what would happen if a superpowerful demon were able to create a dreamlike world to entice people in their own minds. In this dreamlike world, these people were able to access only their minds (which to Descartes included their senses), but not their bodies.[13] Would this dreamlike world be real? Descartes decided that it could not be real, no matter what their perceptions (minds) may tell them; it must be imaginary because all they can be sure of is their physical essences (bodies).[14] In other words, it's not what we can *perceive* that matters in our knowing about the world; it's what we can *touch*. Even though we might be able to see, hear, and smell in a dream, our senses or minds or souls ultimately would be misleading us. Descartes' ideas about the world not only separated the mind from the body but also ascribed to each of them two different properties. Only the body is capable of interacting with the real world; the soul cannot. Thus Western society came to believe there is a disconnection between what is real (what we can prove by physical experimentation) and what is imaginary (what we see or perceive in our hearts or our minds' eye). While Descartes' ideas were cutting-edge philosophy in the seventeenth century, the idea that we cannot know anything outside of our physical experience is not always helpful, especially for people of faith (Heb. 11:1).[15]

Descartes' ideas about the way we can know about our world are so powerful that they underpin all modern Western thought. To make matters worse, Westerners, including well-meaning Christians, take Descartes' ideas for granted as the right way to speak of the mind and the body.[16] In other words, because of the way Westerners are raised and educated, they learn from an early age that it is what we experience in the body that is the primary form of reality (or more specifically, how we know something is real). When Westerners become Christians, they must unlearn this viewpoint to a certain degree as they begin to make room for God's agency and providence that most times cannot be "proven real" with physical evidence.[17] Therefore, when we talk about presence, the

Western worldview influences our understanding and holds that being present — existing somewhere or somewhen, aware of your environment and relating to it — is a *physical* activity.[18] As we discuss presence in both physical and virtual worlds, we Westerners must remember that we have been taught to evaluate our sense of presence (and by extension, how we relate to other people, and by extension, our understanding of community) through Descartes' lens of the world, not a neutral or biblical lens.[19]

Descartes' tremendous influence resulted in a set of laws that govern the Western understanding of presence that ushered in the modern era but are starting to unravel at the beginning of the twenty-first century. Critics unwittingly use these laws in their arguments against virtual churches, even though these arguments are rooted in the values of the modern worldview, not biblical values. If we follow the standard modern view of what it means to be present (the physical experience of somewhere or somewhen), it means that my prayer life, telephone conversations, watching astronauts in outer space, and online gaming are all imaginary experiences that aren't real because I can't experience them in full with my body.[20] In other words, even though I can perceive them, they are not mediated by my body, and hence, according to the Western worldview, I cannot know with certainty whether they are real or illusory.[21] Let me give some examples to ponder to ascertain our immersion in the modern Western worldview. What does it mean to be present at church?

> If I come to worship service on Sunday morning but spend the whole time thinking about the Dallas Cowboys' upcoming football game that afternoon, am I present?
>
> If I go to a megachurch and sit in seat 84K in the mezzanine and watch the pastor on an overhead LCD TV, am I present?
>
> If I am working in the nursery at my church during the service and hear the pastor over the piped-in speaker system, am I present?

If I break my leg and am stuck in the hospital on Sunday morning, but pray for the pastor's message during the service and listen to it over the radio, am I present? (Be careful with this one; more than the others, it will reveal just how much you have been conditioned by modern philosophy rather than the Bible [Col. 2:5; cf. 2 Cor. 5:6 – 9; 12:2 – 3].)

If I break my leg and am stuck in the hospital on Sunday morning, but I have my laptop and log in to Second Life and attend services at the Anglican Cathedral, am I present?

To all — according to the Bible, but not necessarily the modern worldview — the answer is yes. Although, interestingly enough, the first example is the least biblical and the most Western — and the one many readers will give the strongest yes to.

One of the big problems with our learned Western view of presence, besides the fact it's abiblical, is that it doesn't take into account how modern methods of communication, especially computer-mediated communication, can create new forms of experience that are not limited to purely physical interaction.[22] To take these methods into account and try to explain the evolving view of presence, recent thinkers coined the term *telepresence*. Telepresence is typically defined as being present at a spatial or geographical distance through the help of technology. That being said, the concept of telepresence is not at all a more biblical view of presence; rather, it is a recent attempt to tweak or correct the modern Western view of presence to better take into account technologically enhanced experiences that don't fit Descartes' ideal. Without the idea of telepresence, the modern Western viewpoint could not justify how people can know (prove or experience) that men walked on the moon, or have meaningful email conversations. As a result, the concept of telepresence is starting to generate a lot of theological interest, because we could consider God's presence in our churches as a type of spiritual telepresence that would communicate well to educated Westerners. (After all, we consider God to be fully present during worship, despite his not being physically present [Eph. 2:22].) We who were weaned on a strict diet of Western modernism quickly forget that we can pray for someone halfway round the world, and it's real, even though we can't fully understand it, because our spiritual agency, like a reflection of God's, is not limited to our physical space (Matt. 18:18; 1 Cor. 14:32). Someone may say, "Just because a person prays for someone halfway round the world doesn't mean the person praying is *present* with the other person." This is true from the Western ideal. Yet while the person praying is not "there" in body, what about in spirit? If we say to someone, for example, "My thoughts and prayers are with you," is it just a platitude, or do we really mean it? What if by the Spirit's agency we know (or experience) something about the person for whom we are praying while we are praying? Are we present? These types of questions raise incredibly complex and nuanced issues about presence, knowing, and human agency, yet my point here is merely to show the inadequacy of the modern Western ideal (John 17:20–26; Matt. 28:20b). From Moses to Balaam to Paul, the Bible is full of situations that challenge the modern view of presence and force us to reconsider our modern ideas (Rev. 1:10; 2 Cor. 12:2–3; Exod. 12:32; Numbers 23–24). The virtual world gives us the chance to rediscover presence, and community, for the twenty-first century.[23]

P2P Communities

The heart of computer-mediated communication and virtual-world interaction is P2P (peer-to-peer) communication. In essence, peer-to-peer communication occurs when one person connects to one or more people. In the virtual world, a networked node allows for almost unlimited peer-to-peer communication. A networked node is the essence of church community as well. Regardless of our individual definitions of church, no one defines church without including people. One of the minimums for an authentic church is that people (and God) are present. Once people and God are present, a church community becomes possible.

We have seen that people really can be present in a virtual world; therefore, if we and other people come together and are present in the same place in the virtual world, we can create real community. This real community allows for the possibility of a real church, and for a real God to be present with us. (Or to be more theologically accurate, we should say that God's Spirit goes before us into the virtual world; we just meet him there.) Whether we use avatars or chat rooms or holographic virtual reality doesn't matter; what matters is that we are presently united in community under the headship of God for the purpose of worship, fellowship, discipleship, ministry, or evangelism.

Küng reminds us, "An *ekklesia* is not something that is formed and founded once and for all and remains unchanged; it becomes an *ekklesia* by the fact of a repeated concrete event, people coming together and congregating, in particular congregating for the purpose of worshipping God."[24] This is true no matter our ecclesiology. We become the church, the community, the people of God when we become present together, in the presence of God.

From Virtual to Local

Not only can people congregate in the virtual world, constituting a real community of God by their real presence, but this community in the virtual world is a *local* church. I know, some of you already think I am off my rocker, and this seals it, but whether it is the Church of the Simple Faith or ALM Cyberchurch or Flamingo Road Internet Campus, each virtual community is a local church of Christ.

How can a virtual church be local? Glad you asked. If you look the word *local* up in the dictionary, it means "belonging to or existing in a particular place," or more specifically "of or belonging to the

What is real community? While this question is beyond the scope of this book, we can at least briefly lay out several ideas as they relate to virtual churches. Up front, I should say that I'm not equating my use of *community* with any one biblical word from the original languages; rather, I am trying to use it in light of all instances of community in the Bible. As such, virtual churches can fit a biblical definition of real, healthy communities.

This does not mean that all Christian groups of people on the internet qualify as real, healthy communities. Perhaps a better way to say it is that not all Christian communities are created equal. For example, being present seems to be a necessary ingredient for real community. In this instance, telepresence serves, because telepresent worshipers are gathered in the same time and place, but if a worshiper shows up at a church website podcast, since there is no way to know if and when anyone else was ever there, there is no group presence and therefore no community. The church with the podcast could argue that it was creating community with the podcast, but the form of community a podcast creates seems far away from real, healthy community. (Likewise, community built only by email or letter is not exactly community in its fullest sense.) In the same way, it is safe to say that a necessary ingredient of healthy, biblical community is participation. If a group of people all show up at a website but cannot in any way interact, then community doesn't really exist.

Another example we could speak of is positive and negative forms of community. As Christians, we see a coven as a negative form, and a small group as a positive form. But a small group that flirts with witchcraft slides sharply negative. In the same way, virtual churches that proclaim an orthodox gospel and whose members walk with each other as Jesus walked is a positive form of community, whereas a Christian chatroom that often veers from prayer into gossip is a more negative type of community. In contrasting websites and podcasts with virtual churches, it may be that for virtual churches to be healthy forms of Christian community, they must be positive forms in which people are present and participate.

LifeChurch.tv's internet campus, with a multitude of connective applications enabling telepresent community for people from Oklahoma to Pakistan.

neighborhood."[25] In English vernacular, we associate locality with spatiality and geography, but they are not the same thing.[26] We see this happen all the time: if we ask most people to describe their local churches to us, most of them would respond, "It's the place *where* ..." Or worse, "It's the building where ..."[27] But isn't a church supposed to be more about who and what and why than where? Regardless of our opinions on virtual churches, we need to demote the power of the "where" when it comes to being the church.[28] Local churches are local not because of geography but because they are one specific group belonging to a place of seeking after God together.

A virtual church is a local church because it is a place, a specific group of people present together under the headship of Jesus. W. D. Davies points out that Jesus emancipated the people of God from Israel's geographically tied theology (John 4).[29] Being a real church is not tied to or limited by geography, and therefore neither is the local aspect of church. We see this clearly in the letters of Paul. Paul seems to distinguish local churches not by strict geography or physical address but by loose assumptions of locality. So Paul never wrote to the church on Mulberry Street; instead, he wrote to the church in Corinth or Rome, even though there was more than one church in each of those cities. When he wrote to the church at Colossae or Ephesus, he was more than likely referring to lots of individual churches.[30] Further, in the original language, Paul doesn't say "the church of Corinth," as we do in English, but instead he writes literally "to the church of God, the one being in Corinth" (1 Cor. 1:2). What constitutes a church's locality is the *presence* (being) of the community, the people and their God.

Reconsidering the traditional understanding of presence has become even more important in our age of mass transit. Even though Berryessa Valley Church is not a megachurch, I am constantly surprised by the people who come to church regularly or even semi-regularly from as far away as San Francisco or Oakland. To be honest, it doesn't make any sense geographically, but they still come to be present (in community) with us and they are a part of our local church. Some may suggest that their gathering with us in the same physical location is what constitutes a local church, because unlike a virtual church, the people all assemble in the same physical space, but to define a local church this way means we are still defining church in terms of a physical location or a building, not to mention forgetting that virtual worlds are real synthetic spaces. John Hammett explains that the Bible is flexible in its view of a local church since it refers to both house churches and citywide churches as churches, but that "each local congregation is fully *ekklesia* in itself."[31] House churches and citywide churches have different geographical and spatial properties, but they are both local churches.

People come from all over the world to be present and be a part of community at virtual churches such as i-church and St. Pixels. These virtual churches don't exist as churches in geographical terms, but they are local bodies of believers that exist in synthetic places. These synthetic places are rapidly becoming twenty-first century agoras from which all sorts of communities (sacred and secular) spring.[32] These new virtual agoras are driven not only by people's need for authentic community but also by their desire for a real local place that they can call home and have a great deal of ownership. Walter Brueggemann has talked about the growing desire of modern people to possess not just "anarchic space" but "meaningful place" — a real need we see playing out in virtual worlds.[33] What we have, then, are people who, for whatever reason, are moving into the virtual world, where they are really present, forming authentic church communities and establishing local places where together they can be the people of God.[34] They are "the church of God, the one being in Second Life" (or any other region of the virtual world), and each are fully *ekklesia* in themselves.

Virtual Community Protocol

A common concern associated with telepresent church communities is that they will hurt people by encouraging individualism and isolationism.[35] There is a great fear in some segments of society that any increase in the influence of the virtual world in our lives will make our lives worse, not better. Well-meaning Christians and church leaders sometimes express the fear that people will choose to sit in little dark rooms peering into their computer screens rather than engage with real life, or that people will live more and more fractured lives apart from other people and any hope of a real, redeeming church community.[36] But is this true? Probably not as such. The problem is that underlying this claim is a fundamentally flawed assumption, the assumption that in some golden past, the world was less fractured and less isolated than it is today, and that technology is contributing to the worsening of the world. Typically, this way of thinking idealizes the village as a real community, the city as disjointed and broken, and the virtual world as nothing more than *Pinocchio*'s Pleasure Island.[37] The problem with this underlying assumption is that each epoch of human history has different strengths and weaknesses when it comes to developing community; villages may have kept people close, but agrarian ruralism produced its own form of ingrown isolationism.[38] Only God knows whether the world is trending better or worse, and dubious interpretations of Revelation notwithstanding, he's not telling us. It is probably impossible to say whether the virtual world will improve people and communities, or harm them as some well-meaning people claim. In all likelihood, virtual communities will hurt them in some areas and improve them in others. There will be trade-offs, as with everything humanity creates.

There is a very real possibility that virtual-church communities could improve connections between believers. Virtual communities could trump urbanization by allowing vibrant villages of people to congregate in the virtual world. Just as earlier communications technologies such as the telephone "brought people together," so too is it quite possible that the virtual world will bring the church together. At this early point, studies show mixed results: people who use the virtual world for worship seem to grow in community, whereas people who use the virtual world for sinful pursuits tend to become more isolated.[39] Would we expect any different?

Creating community is hard, whether in the real or the virtual world. At the real-world church I pastor, we have invented a radical, superpowerful engine of community-creation. We call it the potluck. Potluck creates community, but it doesn't create the kind of community that people are really craving, the kind of community that exemplifies a genuine church. It is not enough for virtual churches to rely on the connective power of computer-mediated communication to build community. In this, Douglas Groothuis is correct: virtuality cannot "beguile us into mistaking connectivity for community."[40] Potlucks and computer-mediated communication are fabulous for getting people to connect, but we cannot stop there. Virtual churches must develop ways to create community, even if that means using real-world resources to do it. Again, it's not the machine that matters; it's the people.

One danger of virtual connection without virtual community is the unintentional creation of imaginary communities. In this context, an imaginary community is one where a person logs in to what they believe is a community with active participants, but in reality, it is an empty space because they are the only one present at the time.[41] A prevalent example of this is real-world churches, such as Lakeland Church, that use static streaming technologies on their websites to recreate their real-world worship services, or virtual churches such as VirtualChurch.com that offer programmed and choose-your-own-adventure types of worship services. (VirtualChurch.com boasts over 365 billion different possible worship-service combinations.) While we may applaud the power of streaming technology and random number generators to deliver unique, on-demand sermons and worship services, those technologies do not foster community. (You can be present, but you'll be alone.) There are differences between watching a worship service saved on the Lakeland Church website (no community), tuning in to a LifeChurch.tv Internet Campus broadcast service with optional forum (some, perhaps limited, community), and taking part in the Anglican Cathedral in Second Life ("everything but the potluck" community).

We can demonstrate these differences by playing the disruptive cad. There is nothing I can do to mess up the Lakeland Church webcast; it's fixed, it's a performance, it's like TV, I'm an observer. I can sort of disrupt the LifeChurch.tv experience for others by shouting offensive statements in the forum lobby, but I can't affect the worship service itself. I can trash the worship service at Anglican Cathedral if I want by yelling all sorts of boorish things, since I am really present, and other people are really present, and the pastor is really

IS AN INTERNET CAMPUS THE SAME THING AS A VIRTUAL CHURCH?

x

For the most part, yes, although not everyone uses the term *internet campus* in the same way. In North America, a small but rapidly growing number of churches are creating virtual churches following the multisite church model. Instead of planting a stand-alone virtual church, these churches are creating a virtual church that is just one of the mother church's several sites. Early examples of this approach to virtual church include LifeChurch.tv and Flamingo Road Church, both of which have multiple sites for worship services in the real world and in the virtual world.

An internet campus is a virtual church as long as it fits a reasonable definition of church. In contrast to LifeChurch.tv and Flamingo Road, some churches claim to have internet campuses, but these campuses do not appear to fit the definition of a virtual church; the best example of these are churches that stream their recorded services 24/7. Of course, there is nothing inherently wrong with streaming or podcasting; we can liken this to watching TV evangelism or listening to recorded sermons. But since neither watching a TV worship service nor listening to a podcast of a famous pastor's sermon creates community, neither of these examples qualify as churches. In this sense, labeling a podcast an internet campus is misleading. Interestingly, Flamingo Road Church has a broadcast TV worship service (with on-screen forum comments) and an internet campus, but they don't consider the broadcast TV service a campus or a church, though they do consider the internet campus a church. The difference? Community.

Internet campuses are virtual churches in the sense that they use computer-mediated communication to build telepresent Christ communities. They are virtual churches in the sense that they can teach the Bible, administer the sacraments, and practice church discipline. They are not virtual churches, however, if they are just individuals in imagined communities. What sets internet campuses apart from broadcasting or streaming — and makes them virtual forms of the church — is the telepresence of the people of God.

present. Other people can tell me to be quiet, and the pastor can ask me to leave the cathedral, same as in a real-world church.[42] (If I can get into a real fight in a virtual church, isn't that proof that I am really present in a real church? Or at least a real-church business meeting?)

To create not just real but healthy Christian community in the virtual world, the church at large must find ways to distinguish between discipleship materials (streamed messages and podcast services) and actual churches (regular gatherings of real people proactively being the church in the virtual world). This especially appears to be true with the growing trend of internet campuses. Without this distinction, many people may experience increased isolationism and individualism through a misunderstanding of what constitutes community in the virtual world. The less participatory the virtual church, the greater the likelihood that a person will multitask during worship and have an interrupted and fragmented church experience, or really no church experience at all. When well-meaning church leaders knock virtual churches, but post blogs and maintain websites to make their sermons available to people, they are actually contributing to that which they think they are preventing — online community. Except that this type of online community is so impoverished by its lack of participation and interaction as to work against healthier forms of community found in either real-world or virtual-world churches.

If a virtual church is not just a broadcast but a real community united by calling, it has the potential to revolutionize community, to tear down the walls of isolationism and individualism. Think about it: as a real-world pastor, I get maybe two hours per week of being-present time to help build biblical community at my church. The average person gets even less. Part of the problem, of course, is that most people incorrectly perceive of church as the place where a service occurs. I'm a realist, though, so in the real world, I don't tilt much at that windmill. On the other hand, virtual churches have the power to skewer this perception once and for all. We see the popularity (and the power) of social networking sites like MySpace, Facebook, and Twitter and how regularly connected their users are. A virtual church never closes, is potentially active 24/7 as members stay logged-in at work, around the home, or at school in order to support, listen to, pray for, encourage, discuss with, and love others in their networked church community. Most virtual-church pastors I have spoken to emphasize the deeply relational aspects of their jobs. For the first time since maybe Acts 2, we have a form of church that could come very close to being the church rather than just doing church.

As I mentioned in the previous chapter, I'm not suggesting that virtual communities can or should replace real-world communities. That's not the issue. Rather, virtual churches are just another type of local church within the greater body of Christ. And just like any community, they have strengths and weaknesses.[43] But when tele-present people come together as a church, God is there.

chapter 4

The Incarnational Avatar

When I first met Enos Andel, I felt like I had met him somewhere before.

He didn't look exactly the way I imagined he would look—close, yes, but not exactly. Enos was about medium height, of average build with a little bit of extra weight from spending too much time in virtual worlds. He had thick, dark brown hair, an unshaven face fading into a scruffy goatee, and clear eyes. Not terribly polished. His face wasn't warm; it usually betrayed a slight annoyance whenever his goings-on slowed down or he had to stop and wait for anything. Impatient, for sure. He was wearing what he always seemed to wear—a dark club shirt and blue jeans with brown sandals.

I first met Enos at a meet-and-greet, which was hectic and not conducive to getting to know him. He was too busy fulfilling the hosts' requests anyway. The second time I met him was at a non-denominational church, but again, he was all business. The third time, he was a bit more receptive; it was during a regular worship service. Enos took part in the worship and afterward made small talk with a few people before his antsyness got the best of him and he departed with barely a wave.

I ran into him at a different nondenominational church about a month or so later. It was late in the day, and the campus, along with all the neighboring streets and buildings, was deserted. The sunlight had already turned grey and cold. He obviously was lost; he had arrived at the church at an irregular hour and was walking to and fro among several different buildings; I suppose he was trying to find someone in charge. In the distance was a grassy spot where several people were sitting by a large water fountain. I watched as Enos made his way toward them.

As I also got closer to the fountain, I could see three attractive young women who seemed to be conversing quietly about the existence of God and other mysteries of the universe. I don't know how much Enos could hear of their conversation as he approached, but one of the women, who identified herself as a skeptic, got up and walked toward him. She was physically striking, to say the least — tall, thin, proportional, long dark hair with blue highlights, blue eyes. She stopped short of him but said nothing. Enos paused in front of her and the women stopped their conversation. He also said nothing, at least nothing that I could hear. A moment passed. I couldn't read his mind, but I'm willing to bet that for that brief moment he was at a disconcerting multidimensional crossroads. Then, for whatever reason, Enos nodded to the women without saying a word, turned, and headed up the road away from the fountain and the church's empty campus.

The last time I saw Enos was a week later when we happened to visit a Greek Orthodox church at the same time. It was a cold day, snowing outside, giving the church's Byzantine architecture an almost mystical quality. Enos was inside, absorbed with the exquisite icons which were arranged from floor to ceiling on the walls of the church. I left him there, and I don't think he noticed I had left the building.

I am Enos Andel. Enos Andel is my avatar on Second Life. Whether he is more me or I am more him I still don't know. Where he and I go from here remains to be seen.

Being the church in the virtual world means entering the virtual world, and to enter and navigate a virtual world requires a person to make use of and even in some sense become an avatar. When I am present and take part in the community of a virtual church, I do so as an avatar. Millions of people on our planet spend almost as much time living as avatars as they do working, shopping, sleeping, or eating. Studies suggest that in the next decade, most people living in developed countries will make regular use of avatars for everyday activities.[1] If we want to reach people in the virtual world, we have to reach avatars, even though the whole avatar thing gives a lot of church people the willies.

Can avatars know God? Can the people of God experience spiritual growth as avatars?

Virtual Identity

In the last chapter, I explained that when people enter virtual worlds, their presence is real, though not in the modern Western worldview's rigid sense of the idea. We are present in virtual worlds through the extension of ourselves by way of computer-mediated communication, and it is our presence that permits virtual communities to exist and thrive. Still, it's not quite that simple, because there are layers of separation between us and other people in virtual worlds.[2] One of the most prominent layers is each individual's use of an avatar for self-representation and even for identity formation. Since an avatar is the only conduit by which virtual community is built, the avatar stands "at the center of virtual worlds."[3]

In the virtual world, an avatar is at its root a "representation of the self within a [virtual] environment."[4] When I enter into a 3D virtual world like Second Life, I can see myself as an avatar, and this is also the way other residents of Second Life see me. My avatar is a high-resolution, fully customizable figure that represents me as I choose to be represented in the virtual world. However, there is more to it than just that. An avatar also represents the possibility of a new identity — a possibility that many people choose to exercise. For some people, an avatar is simply a tool to be used to get a job accomplished — like using a shovel. When I first joined Second Life, my impulse was to create an avatar that was, basically, "me." (Kinda boring, I know.) But for others, there is a desire to create avatars very much unlike their real-world selves, and a desire to create and role-play the identity of their differentiated avatars. For them, an avatar becomes almost another person — like a whole new identity.

Think of it like this: on Sundays, after I lead the morning services at my real-world church, I am acutely aware as I go out to lunch with folks from church that not only am I Douglas but I am also Pastor Douglas. Even though I don't consider "pastor" to be my true identity, people speak to me as if it is my true identity. And in most cases I speak back to them wearing my "pastor's cap," rather than, say, how I may want to speak to them. This parallel holds in virtual worlds, since people not only will choose and use an avatar that is a bodybuilder or an elf or a toaster oven but often will choose to act — or sometimes, more precisely, to live — as if they are a bodybuilder or an elf or a toaster oven.

Let me give a more specific example. When I inhabit Second Life, I take on the identity of and become Enos Andel. When people speak to me, they address me as Enos, not Douglas. When I go to church, people say, "Hi, Enos!" I may pick out Enos's clothes and decide where

Enos goes, but his identity is distinct from my own. This becomes even more apparent for people who have more than one avatar; people with multiple avatars naturally tend to create distinct identities for each avatar.

While some people may never go to the extent of creating avatars with new and divergent personalities, it is true that the more real avatars seem, the more likely people are to form basic identities for them.[5]

The Meat-Free Life

William Gibson, the science-fiction author of *Neuromancer* and the coiner of the word *cyberspace*, calls our virtual forms "data made flesh."[6] Another way of saying this is that our presence in the virtual world must be encased in some sort of "body," just as our hearts, minds, and souls are "encased" in a physical body in the real world.[7] Virtual-world inhabitants use this body not only to represent themselves but also to form an identity for other people to see. This is the type of pseudospiritual language that makes some church people feel funny about virtual worlds. But it doesn't matter. Here's why. If you're reading this book, no matter what you may feel about avatars, you already have at least one. In fact, 98 percent of you reading this book already have multiple avatars. Weird, huh? Watch, I'll prove it.

The internet and the virtual world get a bad rap as if somehow disembodied meat-free brains are floating around in some type of weird electronic ether, but that's sci-fi, not reality.[8] When a person logs in to a virtual world, that person becomes telepresent in a networked community. For that to happen, the person cannot be some kind of "pure mind"; humans don't work that way. Instead, that person has to have a "virtual body" — an avatar — to typify them and differentiate them from other people in the community. The avatar identifies them to others in the virtual world.

If you have an email address, you have an avatar.

Whether your email address is douglas@simchurch.com or ilovemillivanilli@gmail.com, your email address is a rudimentary representation of you within a virtual environment. On a basic level, it forms a virtual identity. It's the most basic of avatars. Some of the first avatars were even more modest. When virtual worlds first came on the scene, researchers and scientists needed a way to identify themselves in text-based worlds, and so they created labels that would do just that. Think of them as "handles" from a bad 1970s trucker movie. Without these handles or avatars, computer-mediated communication would be impossible. As virtual worlds evolved from simple text-based bulletin boards to 2D representations still popular on forums to 3D spaces such as Second Life, so did the quality of the representation of the self, and so did the ability to create identity. What we refer to today as avatars developed from handles to stylized GIFs to full-body, high-resolution representations. With each evolution came not only more power to shape our virtual identities but also more uncertainty among those for whom the technology seemed foreign.

Let's face it, one of Christians' biggest dilemmas with becoming an avatar is that the word *avatar* originates from a non-Christian religion. The original meaning of the word contradicts our belief system. *Avatar* is from the Sanskrit meaning "descent," and in Hindu theology, it's the word for the descent and embodiment of a deity in human form. Thus, Krishna and Rama are two important avatars of the same god, Vishnu, who came to earth in human form. Christians, though, don't believe in avatars; we deny them. Jesus, the Messiah, was not an avatar because he didn't come to earth as an embodiment of deity. Jesus is the Messiah because God the Son became in every way human without in any way ceasing to be deity (John 1:14). He wasn't embodied as a human; he was human. We call this an incarnation, not a descent, because Jesus didn't put on flesh; he became flesh. By the way, we can often see divine descent in Hindu religious art — scenes with people engaged in various activities among whom there is one or more divine avatars. The divine avatar is frequently represented differently than regular folks; for example, one of the avatars of Vishnu, Krishna, radiates with a dark blue color to let viewers know that this is a divine being encased in human flesh. In the virtual world, an avatar simply lets other people know a person, not an object, is there; it's just a handle, sign, representation, or signature that helps to create identity. There is nothing unbiblical or un-Christian about a person using an avatar to worship God in a virtual church.

Still, some will be unconvinced. This mind-out-of-body idea, which has a lot more to do with our learned sense of what it means to exist than with a biblical perspective, continues to haunt virtual churches.[9] Some traditionalists have bought into the notion that virtual churchgoers want to leave their bodies behind. It seems like every time I come across a blog or forum discussing virtual churches, without fail someone always posts a response claiming virtual churches and worshiping as an avatar are just modern forms of Gnosticism.

Are they, though?

Not really. We often hear Christian people link modern-day movements with which they disagree with ancient heresies. In a few cases, there is good reason and the parallel holds. In this case, though, there are all sorts of problems with comparing the practice and theology of virtual churches to Gnostic thought. The biggest difficulty is that there really isn't such a thing as Gnostic thought per se; Gnosticism is a highly publicized but poorly understood and poorly delineated hodgepodge of ideas that's long on generalities and short on particulars.[10] To say that telepresent worship is somehow related to an ancient cult of people who wanted to free their divine spirits from the prisons of their evil bodies in order to float through space battling demons to get to God is hardly accurate.

Using technology to facilitate communication and presence is a far cry from repudiating all flesh. Really, there are no theological or practical parallels between Gnosticism and any of the more mainstream virtual churches and internet campuses; almost all of these churches borrow their theologies and proclamation models from mainstream Protestant practice.

A better and more thoughtful concern is the question of whether virtual churches foster a more Platonic form of Christianity. The thinking of Plato undergirds almost everything Westerners believe; whether or not they realize it or want to admit it, more Western Christians base their worldview on his philosophy than on any purely biblical philosophy. Plato's thinking influenced important Christian theologians such as Augustine, Athanasius, and Thomas Aquinas, each of whose thinking underlie many modern theologies. When it came to personhood, Plato believed that people belong to two different worlds — a physical world of dynamic change and a heavenly world of static ideals. He believed that a person's soul belongs more to the heavenly world, the superior world, and a person's body belongs to the physical world, the inferior world that we live in now. Plato, along with his later followers, such as Plotinus, didn't deny the physical world; he simply privileged ideas over actions.

As more and more people move into and take up residence in the virtual world, creating more and more detailed and personalized avatars, a growing temptation will be to further Platonize the church by privileging our minds and souls over our physical bodies.[11] We could see this play out with great discussion and emphasis on idealized personal morality rather than social action or hands-on ministry. However, an orthodox biblical theology of the body doesn't privilege the soul over the body; according to the Bible, our bodies, minds, souls, and hearts are all part of what makes us persons.[12] There are qualitative differences but not substantive distinctions. We don't have eternal (pre-existent) souls; we are "embedded in creation as creatures," created by God,[13] able to be redeemed and spend the remainder of eternity in his neighborhood, but this is due to God's grace, not the inherent property or value of our souls. In fact, our bodies are just as redeemable as our souls (Rom. 8:23) and are the temporary dwelling places of God on earth (1 Cor. 6:19), an idea that Plato would consider preposterous. No matter how steeped the Western psyche is in the philosophies of Plato and Descartes, these philosophies betray us when we try to fit God's church into them.

If virtual churches run the risk of privileging minds and souls over bodies, it won't be because of a philosophical agenda but rather because every iteration of the church has different strengths and weaknesses. On a given Sunday at my real-world church, my worship team and I don't have any problem engaging people with their bodies — people sing, dance, speak, wave. What we worry about is whether we are engaging them in worship with their hearts and minds,[14] and like many pastors and leaders of real-world churches, we design our services accordingly. Anecdotal evidence suggests that, on average, people who attend virtual-world churches are at least as connected in mind and heart as in a typical real-world church, and so virtual-world churches will have to design their churches to engage the *bodies* of their people. The Bible tells us that we are to glorify God with our bodies (1 Cor. 6:20; cf. Rom. 12:1), something that is quite possible and reasonable in any healthy virtual church, but that will take extra effort to do. Whether we are in a real-world or virtual-world church, we are called to help people love and serve God with all of their hearts, souls, minds, and strength (Luke 10:27).

Multiverse Masks

Now that we have come to terms with the nature of avatars, we must ask, What role will they play in virtual churches? At the beginning of this chapter I asked the question, Can avatars know God? No. Because avatars aren't people, they can't worship, can't be discipled, and can't find salvation — not as such. At face value, an avatar is a symbol — a person's name and identity in the virtual world. However, while it is true that avatars can't know God (because they are merely pixilated representations and identities of real people), it is true that a person can create an avatar that has an identity of knowing God. In other words, a Second Life Satanist who gets bored with a Satanist avatar could decide one day to create a Christian avatar. The Satanist may go so far as to speak and act as a Christian and pretend to know God through the avatar. So in a sense, avatars can worship, can be disciples, and can find salvation — through the real person behind them or through the avatar's identity (which may or may not be indicative of valid worship, discipleship, or salvation), but strictly speaking it is impossible for the avatar to receive salvation; the person who acts as the avatar must take that step.

But I also asked a second question: can the people of God experience spiritual growth as avatars? This question is not so simple to answer.[15] The people whom those avatars represent can worship, be discipled, and find salvation, and they can do so while in avatar form. In fact, people who worship God as avatars can worship God as easily as people who worship without avatars in the real world. (Remember, people in the real world have other modes of representation; we'll talk about this more in chapter 7.) The virtual world is brimming with avatars, through which people are able to glorify God with their first and second lives, and numerically speaking, it's the most unchurched place on earth. Let's do something about it.

When a person creates a sign, a handle, a name, a representation, and an identity for themselves, it becomes a *part* of them. Not in some intrinsic sense of their very existence, but symbolically. This is true in the real world. We value our names, our favorite clothes or personal effects; they help us to carve out a distinctive identity. If I wake up tomorrow and find out that the powers that be have sold my website or my email address without my consent, I will be torqued to the nth degree. They *stole* MY virtual identity. Most of us don't even want to lose our cell phone number when we move. Right now, there is a certain amount of disposability of avatars among certain populations, but that will steadily decrease in the future for most people,[16] and the more popular that high-quality, 3D avatars become, the more we will see them as natural extensions of ourselves.[17] They will form a significant part of our personal identities, certainly online, but offline as well.[18] For most people born into the digital generation, even the prospect of losing their avatars is very painful.[19] The closer the representation is to our essence, the more we see it as an extension of ourselves; just as I care more about douglas@simchurch.com than ilovemillivanilli@gmail.com, so will most people care a great deal more about a highly realistic, trans-virtual-world representation of themselves. In fact, in some cultures such as South Korea, avatar customization has already become big business, with some people spending thousands of dollars on creating the perfect avatar with the latest avatar fashions.

Sensationalistic news reports make us believe that everyone on the internet is faking their identities and hiding behind screen names or avatars. Yet we all know that the news in general focuses on the aberration, the 2 percent; every pastor of a virtual church that I spoke to found the fakes to be the exception rather than the rule in their experience. Still, I'm not denying it — there will always be a few mischievous people who want to hide their identities and disrupt the party for everyone else, and there will always be those who are less than forthcoming. Would we expect anything different? No, because we encounter the same identity issues in the real world. In the real world, just as in the virtual world, there are people who want to hide their identities for less than ethical reasons and people who choose to hide certain aspects of their identities. For example, I'll bet you anything that scores of people in your real-world church hide their true spiritual identities in their day-to-day lives; they go to work, go to the mall, go out for dinner, go walking in the park, and most if not all of the people they meet have no idea whether they are followers of Christ (or Loki, for that matter). Many Westerners hide behind middle-class prudence and acceptability. Even pastors at times mask our identities by buying homes outside of our church's suburb so we don't run into church members at the grocery store. It is safe to say that there are (and will be) identity issues in every world populated by humans.[20] In contrast to all this, the virtual world does make it easy to make it clear in a nonthreatening and honest way that I'm living my life for Jesus; anyone who accesses my avatar's profile knows that I am a Second Life Christian and a member of several virtual churches. I could hide it, but it's just as easy not to. Masks can both hide and proclaim identity. Masks exist in both the real and virtual worlds. (We'll talk more about this in chapter 7.)

Lifelogging for Jesus

As we encounter the next wave of the digital revolution, sophisticated or intelligent lifelogging will be at the forefront. Lifelogging is "the capture, storage and distribution of everyday experiences and information for objects and people."[21] Several generations ago, lifelogging involved writing family members' birth, wedding, and death dates into the family Bible. Today, some of the lifelogging we do is intentional: blogs we write or personal websites we create. However, computers record a great deal of additional information about every one of us. Whether we realize it or not, our emails, our uploaded photos, our forum posts all record our lives for future generations. Your great-great-grandchildren will know how you felt about this book by your Amazon review of it.[22] To be honest, I don't have a clue what the names of any of my great-great-grandparents are, much less what books they read and liked (or hated). How will the prospect of perpetual lifelogging affect how we live our lives and be the church?

If you ask the average person whether it is easier to wear a mask in the real world or the virtual world, almost everyone will say the virtual world; the news media and salacious anecdotes have convinced them of this. As we've discussed, this is not necessarily true and probably will become less and less true as future technology arrives. My virtual presence records facts about me that are hard to mask. In Second Life, anyone I befriend can find out when I'm online and where I am. ("A virtual church … umm, I was just sightseeing.") On Fatwallet.com, anyone who knows my handle can see I left a positive star for someone who had posted a sale at a Christian bookstore. ("Hey, it just sounded like a good deal!") On MySpace, any friend from church can post "Jesus loves you!" for the world to see. ("Oh, well, yes, I have some religious friends … doesn't everyone?")

In the real world, we challenge people to live lives that are consistent with the gospel of Jesus Christ. Virtual churches can challenge people the same way in virtual worlds. It is quite possible to live consistently in any world. In both worlds, people are tempted to put on masks in the same ways for the same reasons; the only difference is the quality of the mask.[23] In both worlds, other people will look at our actions and how we live our lives; how we live will shape the faith of many people around us (1 Peter 2:9 – 12). In some ways, the stakes are higher in the virtual world because many of my words and actions are "on file" for anyone to review.

One Second Lifer testifies, "[After joining a virtual church], I found that while my personal desire for using Second Life was the same, I began changing my avatar's 'lifestyle.' I became more aware of where I took my avatar: it was not as comfortable to walk through the clubs and casinos in the areas marked 'adult'; I stopped looking for money-making opportunities on Sundays and instead only stayed logged in to Second Life long enough to attend worship services. It was as if my avatar had made a move to a more Christian lifestyle."[24] This is someone else's testimony; but as we review the logs of our own lives — virtual or real — what do they reveal?

Anyone who ventures online can create powerful lifelogs — testimonies — of their commitment and service to God. While this is possible in the real world, it seems almost automatic for residents of virtual worlds. In contrast to the real world, the virtual world typically allows the average person to demonstrate their faithfulness in a much more consistent way, a way that is demonstrable to others through their lifelogs. To be honest, I don't know if my great-great-grandfather was a believer or not; I don't know about anything that he may or may not have done for the cause of Christ. But my great-great-grandchildren will know about my life — from the recorded data of my life — so I better make it a righteous one.

While we have the power as avatars to speak life to other people as avatars in the virtual world, do our virtual identities say to others "sincere person for Jesus" or "I want to fool around"? Unlike in the real world, how we represent ourselves in the virtual world is both much more obvious and recorded for all to see. Virtual churches need to be impacting people in the virtual world just as real-world churches need to be impacting people in the real world. One excellent way for this to happen is for virtual churches to harness the lifelogged testimonies of virtual Christians as permanent testimonies of God's agency in our world. These testimonies, coupled with the power of telepresence and computer-mediated communication, give virtual churches an unprecedented opportunity to develop fully devoted disciples — and avatars — of Christ.

Fully Devoted Avatars of Christ

Dealing with people is always a double-edged sword. Russell, a twenty-year-old English major at San Jose State University, plays World of Warcraft with his highest-possible-level Orc warrior as much as sixty to eighty hours per week, especially in the summer. I

Enos Andel praying in a virtual church.

asked him about his gameplay one afternoon after lunch. "The best thing about World of Warcraft is the people," he responded. The worst thing? "The worst thing is the people." When we enter virtual worlds, our avatars encounter avatars; for good or bad, those avatars represent and identify real people with real questions looking for real answers.

Bobby Gruenewald, Innovation Pastor at LifeChurch.tv, explains the trade-offs: "What I have found so far is that there are definitely people in Second Life who simply want to hide behind their avatar and say/do things they normally would not say/do in real life. However, it is this same lack of inhibition that leads people to ask questions about God they would not normally feel comfortable exploring in real life. Creating an avatar becomes a very nonthreatening way for people to explore more about God."[25]

To illustrate this openness, let's say I decide one day to share the gospel with people in Second Life. But actually, I can't share it with people. I have to share it with avatars, because that is the identity that people assume in the virtual world. So I share with avatars. When I do so, the avatar that I attempt to share with knows only that Enos Andel is sharing with him or her or it; the person the avatar represents doesn't know who Douglas Estes is and they may never know. (If I set my profile to public, they could.) They may not want to know. This may sound unusual to people who have never ventured into a virtual world, but to reach a person through an avatar, in some situations you still have to reach the avatar first.

So let's say that I'm sharing with an avatar named Anarchy Jones, an avatar of a real-world person named Eric, who is agnostic. In Eric's mind, Anarchy Jones is nihilistic. Eric thought it would be cool to live a life with different rules than he lives by in real life. If I — but it's not I, it's Enos ... If Enos invites Anarchy Jones to church, I don't know who will respond. Eric may be a little open, but Eric is well aware that Anarchy Jones would never darken the door of a church. At that point I have a decision to make: I could try to reach Eric, which may cause him to abandon Anarchy Jones as an avatar and adopt a milder Seeker Jones avatar, who would then try a virtual church, or I may decide a better approach is to throw a Nihilists 4 Jesus party, in which case Eric could decide it would be okay and maybe good for Anarchy Jones to go. Eric, as Anarchy Jones, could hear the gospel that way. But in Eric's mind, Eric is not coming; it is Anarchy Jones who is coming to the party, and it is Anarchy Jones who hears the gospel. In fact, Eric may think it is cool for Anarchy Jones to convert to Christianity and change his avatar to Anarchy4Jesus Jones, even though Eric himself may never convert. Or Eric could convert but still keep a pagan avatar (in which case we speak more of Eric than his avatar, because this is more clearly Eric's problem). This may be an extreme example, but virtual ministry can be as complex as real-world ministry.

Anyone involved in virtual-world ministry knows that people will ask the hard questions, the real questions, the questions that need to be answered, much more freely in the virtual world than in the real world. In a very real sense, this loosening of inhibition could allow a person a starting point for becoming a fully devoted disciple of Christ in the virtual world better than in the real one. But to guide people in this process, authentic virtual churches, not just websites with static (and often outdated) information, are necessary.

As a pastor in the real world, I know that the average attendee at my church won't come to me and bare the depths and depravity of their soul in search of understanding (or commiseration). They won't ask the really hard questions "live." Something about the masks, layers, and representations we acquire in the real world prevents us from that degree of disclosure. Yet these same people will log on to their computer and Google for answers. (Are pastors *really* less trustworthy than Google?) If they are aware of the possibility, they will talk about it over the internet through forums or virtual friends. While no one knows how commonplace this is, researchers believe it is endemic — growing numbers of people of faith, unsatisfied with their churches, are seeking answers in the virtual world.[26] We can all agree this type of spiritual information grazing — Googling for spiritual growth — won't produce disciples. So what will?[27] And if the answer for some of those people is virtual churches, how can virtual churches partner with real-world churches to make it happen?

Avatar Discipleship: Packets or Loops?

Let's consider two different ways that information in computer-mediated communication is handled: packets and feedback loops.[28] In the first way, when two or more computers communicate with each other, the sending computer breaks the outgoing information down into smaller units called packets; the receiving computer receives the packets one at a time and reassembles the information.

WHY NOT WITNESS TO PEOPLE ONLINE AND THEN INVITE THEM TO A REAL CHURCH?

Among people who doubt the validity of virtual churches, a common argument is that the church should use the power of computer-mediated communication to share the gospel with people in virtual worlds, and then invite them to real-world churches. Wouldn't this be the best of both worlds?[a]

No, and it won't work in many situations. First, many people who hold this viewpoint can't or won't distinguish between fictional worlds and virtual worlds. This is important, because they misunderstand the capacity of the virtual world for discipleship. They think of the virtual world as equivalent to broadcast television, when it is a completely different medium.[b] In broadcast television (especially in the form of televangelism), one can hear the gospel and receive salvation, but the potential for spiritual growth is limited, perhaps nonexistent. Since the virtual world is fully participatory, spiritual growth is at least as possible as in the real world.

Second, there are logistical problems that would be nigh on impossible to overcome. If I share the gospel in the virtual world with someone who lives in Cleveland, I can probably recommend a real-world church to them with some confidence. But not if they live in Nuevo Vallarta. Or Kiev. Or Osaka. The average Christian engaged in conversational evangelism doesn't have the resources to connect most individuals with real-world churches; maybe even the Roman Catholic Church lacks those resources. More important, there is no way to ensure that the person from Osaka with whom you've just shared the gospel will actually go to a real-world church. Most times, people just won't go without a friend to accompany them.[c] No matter where in the world a person lives — Nuevo Vallarta, Kiev, Osaka, or even Cleveland — they can go to church with you if you invite them to a virtual church.

Finally, and if I may coin a word here, this argument is based on the flawed premise of "worldism." Think of its close cousin, colonialism: when European missionaries went to African countries to share the gospel, some made the terrible mistake of requiring Africans to learn English (to read the Authorized Version of the Bible) and to sing European hymns instead of empowering Africans to create their own contextualized form of church. The result? Many Africans reject the gospel today because they see it as a European religion.[d] Asking someone whom you've shared the gospel with to leave the familiarity of their virtual world and go to some real-world church with unfamiliar customs is pretty much the same as sharing the gospel with a person from another country and then telling them to start dressing, speaking, and worshiping like you.

That's the reason this argument is a cop-out. Every time I have helped plant a church in Africa, I've seen well-meaning church people from North America doing "crusades" in religious hot spots, such as the slums. If the people listening make a decision, it doesn't seem to matter much because the crusaders are already on a plane back to the US, but this is not what Jesus asks us to do (Matt. 28:18 – 20). Jesus calls us to make disciples, and the most effective way to do that is to plant churches. It is not enough to go into a new world and share the gospel, and then leave the people to their own devices; we have enough hit-and-run evangelism in the real world. The best way to reach and disciple people in virtual worlds is with virtual churches.

------

a. Tim Hutchings points out that some church leaders have gone so far as to close down evangelistic websites so as to force the people to come to their real-world churches; see Tim Hutchings, "Theology and the Online Church," *Epworth Review* 35:1 (2008).

b. This misunderstanding is apparent in Groothuis' work; see Douglas Groothuis, *The Soul in Cyberspace* (Grand Rapids, Mich.: Baker, 1997), 159.

c. One poster on Craig Groeschel and Bryan Gruenewald's blog *Swerve* commented that most of the people with whom he had shared the gospel in the virtual world were interested in Jesus but would never consider attending a real-world church.

d. From my personal experience sharing the gospel in affluent areas of East Africa.

Packeting is an automated, linear method of processing information. In the second way, when a computer receives information (such as a packet), it sends a response to the sending computer. This response immediately changes the next bit of information (such as a packet) sent out by the sending computer, over and over again, creating what is known as a feedback loop. A good (or really devious) example of a feedback loop is the spam cycle. Spammers send out millions of emails broken down into billions of packets; one of those emails will show up in your in-box. If you click the link that says "please remove me from your list" in the spam message, your computer sends this information to the spammer's computer, which adjusts itself to spam you more. This method allows a spammer blindly sending out emails to millions of computers to quickly target email addresses where people are actually taking the time to read and interact with spam they receive. In contrast to packets, a feedback loop is an intelligent, collective, creative method of processing information.

Let's take these ideas about communication and create an analogy for the spiritual growth of people in real-world and virtual-world churches. In my real-world church, most people come to one worship service a week, where they receive their "packet" of information via audio transmission (listening). Week in and week out, these average, real-world churchgoers receive a packet of discipleship information that they take home and try to assemble into their lives. But disruptions such as missed worship services, guest speakers, and poor long-term memory limit the effectiveness of packet-based discipleship. In contrast, every real-world pastor would love to see all of their people get highly involved in a small group. Why? Because this once-a-week group allows people to generate a meaningful "feedback loop" in their lives. When they go to small group and receive a discipleship packet, they can immediately "ping" the small-group leader for further explanation, insight, help, or prayer. Instead of receiving only their weekly packet of information on

Sunday, real-world small-group attendees receive further information via their feedback loop on how to assemble this discipleship information and, hopefully, put it into practice.

Virtual churches have the power to take this one big step farther. Real-world churches are places where we go, and even small groups are places to most people; everything is rooted primarily in the "where." The power of virtual churches is to change the where to the when. Pam Smith, the priest in charge of i-church, feels that virtual churches are more of a continuum than a place. At i-church, virtual churchgoers don't have to wait for their weekly packet of information but instead have their lives integrated into a spiritual feedback loop that is always on.[29] From prayer requests to handling issues to understanding biblical ideas, computer-mediated communication allows a fully devoted disciple of Christ to be constantly engaged by others who attend their church (Prov. 27:17). Virtual churchgoers can link their avatars into their church's spiritual network, where they are connected to a constant biblical and spiritual feedback loop. Lifelogging itself leads to a perpetual feedback loop in which participatory growth experiences can be referenced and rereferenced to facilitate spiritual growth in the virtual churchgoer (or in any seeker, for that matter). To complete the analogy, discipleship as feedback loop instead of packet could be the twenty-first century equivalent of ancient *paideia*, a type of discipleship held by many early church fathers that stressed not just education but formation. Virtual churches can open up a whole new approach to discipleship, "a new mode of synchronous learning."[30]

The good news is that computer-mediated communication will benefit not just virtual-world churches but real-world churches as well. But the reason virtual churches will be needed is that real-world churches, by nature, will not be as adept at establishing a continuum for growth and community. As people increasingly use avatars not only for executing daily tasks and gameplaying but also for spiritual seeking and growth, virtual churches can play a large role in rekindling discipleship and spiritual formation in people's lives. Because of the continual, not spatial, nature of virtual churches, the average virtual churchgoer is likely to be just as committed to their virtual church as the average real-world churchgoer is to their real-world church, though neither iteration of the church is perfect, or even close to it. These ideas will continue to gain traction as post-digital-revolution generations understand better how to use the technology to build a meaningful network of fully lifelogged avatars for Christ.[31]

Hermas' opinion of this new thing called church? Disorganized.

Two years after he had grudgingly agreed to support his wife, Rhoda, and observe the Sabbath with other followers of the Way at a church, instead of at the synagogue of his birth, Hermas was even more torn apart than ever. To him, the synagogue made sense and the church didn't. He struggled with these thoughts as he and his family walked home after leaving the newest place for the church, the house of a Roman tradesman named Sylvus.

It wasn't so much the debate over whether the Galilean Jew Jesus was a rabbi or a prophet or even the Messiah. Hermas could accept all three; he was mostly convinced, and his wife truly believed. And he knew things were different now.

His hometown, Iconium, had always been something of a political cauldron, what with simmering frictions and bubbling hullabaloos regularly arising from the diversity of the populace. But since the followers of the Way had arrived, preaching first in the synagogues and then in the marketplaces, the streets, the wheat fields, and even the orchards, all Hades had broken loose. There had been riots, and last year, some Jewish Zealots had nearly killed one of the leaders of the Way, Rabbi Paul.

Hermas and his family were not at the center of this, but it had spilled over into their Sabbath activities. First they met at Euthalia's house. Then Iddo's. Then several other places before settling, for now, at Sylvus'.

That wasn't the worst part. Church was always disorganized. When the church was at Euthalia's, it was small and loose, but orderly. But as the church in Iconium grew, more churches were started, and there was a great deal of confusion over who was in charge of what. Some Sabbaths, foreign Jews would show up requesting (or demanding) to speak; more than once it had resulted in a shouting match followed by their expulsion. Far worse was when *Greeks* showed up asking to speak. Hermas considered himself cosmopolitan, but this seemed a little too much even for him.

As he and his family continued to walk along the quiet avenue lined with near-ripe apricots, Hermas realized the thing that bothered him the most about the new church was the lack of tradition, the lack of authority. The church at Sylvus' had selected several servant-helpers to tend to families in need, and Iddo was still serving as the church ruler.

The break with Jewish tradition and the synagogue had led to disarray. There was no council, no proper procession of *shema*, and Iddo was a weak ruler, at least in Hermas' eyes.

Most Sabbaths, he wondered whether the church would last until the next week. Somehow, it always did.

chapter 5

WikiWorship

I knew what worship in church is supposed to be like and I was pretty sure this wasn't it.

My first church-planting trip in East Africa with Build the Village was simple. As part of a mixed team of indigenous soon-to-be-pastors and American assistants, we planted several churches right outside of Nairobi, Kenya. Simple, because Nairobi is a high-profile, Western-Christianized, everyone-does-mission-trips-there kind of place.

The second time was different; we planted churches in a poor but low priority rural area outside of the North Meru District near a town called Kianjhai. Most of the people there belong to the Meru tribe — decent, honest folk for the most part — but the most lucrative farming option in the area is *miraa*, an amphetamine-like stimulant, so most good people in the area live in poverty rather than grow or run drugs. If you ask what religion most people are, they will say Christian, but since their primary Christian influence is the God-will-make-you-rich broadcasting network beamed into the local dry-goods shop, the only thing the average person knows about Jesus is that he is a god who can get them money (if they have enough faith).

The Sunday before the launch of four new churches in the tiny villages dotting the remote hilltops, we had our kickoff worship service at the mother church — in a building of sticks in a field barren except for the occasional acacia tree. Everyone was excited; most of the American team members were still in culture shock but adjusting well. The service eventually got underway with greetings and introductions, mostly in Swahili and English, but some in the local Meru dialect, which I didn't know.

In my earlier experiences in Africa, I had gotten a little accustomed to some of the differences between the way people worship in various churches in Nairobi and the way people tend to worship in North America or Western Europe. For example, one of the more difficult adjustments was singing worship music set to a traditional African scale, which sounds grating and unpleasant to many Westerners. Not only was it difficult to adjust to African musical styles, the farther out from civilization we went, the less Western influence there was, and the more difficult it seemed to adjust to worship.

That's exactly what happened that day at the launch church. After the grueling worship set, the pastor of the launch church invited people to pray for the planting of the new churches and for God's favor on our mission. So everyone stood, turned away from each other, and started talking, all at once, out loud — some very loudly — eyes closed, fists in the air, creating a deafening cacophony in this small church of tree limbs and tin roof.

It was startling. It felt very … wrong. I couldn't understand what they were saying because it was all in Kimeru, the local dialect, not Kiswahili or English. I leaned over to my pastor friend from Nairobi and asked him what in the world was going on.

"They're praying," he said.

But not like this, I thought. Their praying wasn't like a few people talking in conversation groups in a library; it was like the roar of an angry mob. Even though there was no one around for miles, I wondered what people outside the church would think of the service.

A thought flitted through my mind: this must be what Dante's inferno sounds like.

As I continued to sit uncomfortably, I watched the people pray for what seemed like forever. I began to make out some Kiswahili loan words (*Mungu Baba*, "Father God"); I began to see tears of repentance. It was the first time in my life I witnessed real lamentation that didn't involve death.

I thought about it all that day. It had been an uncomfortable and downright bizarre time of prayer. Bizarre like traditional African worship music played on electric guitar might seem to Westerners. Bizarre like the smells and bells in liturgical churches might seem to many Africans. Bizarre to me, but maybe not bizarre to God.

The next day, during the morning worship to prepare our teams for day two, prayer time came and I prayed. I prayed, standing, looking into the wall of sticks, shouting, and the only people who existed for an hour were God and me.

●

Everyone, me included, sees the church through a cultural lens — or against someone else's cultural lens — more so than through God's lens or a biblical lens. This is true no matter the biblical prooftexts used or the tradition cited; in fact, it must be true. It must be true because if we declare the church to be of God, then it must in large part be incomprehensible to people who cannot ever come close to understanding God. Until we come to admit that we see the church through our limited, human perspective, and that therefore how we do church originates more from our human ideas than from a divine blueprint from heaven, we will never be able to do church in a way that is more about God than about an organization of our own making. Anything of God is as much a mystery to us fallen people as the incarnation or creation. The church is a mystery; we do the best we can to recreate this mystery. And we are blessed when we do (Ps. 65:4).

More than anything else, our cultural lens influences what we see as the "right" and "wrong" practice of church. Denominationalism, liturgical strictures, parachurch ministries, open versus closed Communion, and worship wars all derive more from our human attempts to formulate the mystery of the church in a reasonable way than from a biblical or divine precept. For most of us, we do church a certain way because that's the way we learned to do church. For the rest of us, we do church against the way we learned to do church, as a reaction against someone else's style of doing church. Some are better and some are worse, perhaps, but none is best.

Virtual churches also must find their own way to do church, and do it well, in the new millennium. It seems likely that culture and technology will push the church at large to become even more "wiki, wiki" (or "faster, faster," as it means in the Hawaiian) — meaning the church, especially virtual churches, will be expected to become more collaborative and decentralized. Some hope that technology will "reform" the practices of the church, but technology doesn't implement itself — people implement it. What will all of this mean for virtual churches, internet campuses, and other tech-heavy forms of church? What will it mean for their core practices?

How will virtual churches change the way we "do" church? Are virtual sacraments and other faith practices possible or valid (or just inevitable)?

As we have seen, most of the confusion over the nature, validity, and strategic significance of virtual churches comes into play not because of theology but mostly because of a misunderstanding of technology and a reliance on a modernist, abiblical philosophy or worldview. At the same time, virtual churches will have to answer some hard questions about their worship practices if they expect to minister shoulder-to-shoulder with churches in the real world. We cannot allow them a pass just because they're new or cool or because all the other kids are doing it.

Faith Service Providers

Virtual churches are slowly but surely coming out of their shells — the shells of the real-world traditions that launched them. We can see some parallels here with the Protestant Reformation. After the unforeseen but irreparable split with Rome, Luther and the early Reformers found themselves with a need for a new kind of church. Working out a better, more biblical theology for the church was a high priority, but what they did not immediately seek to do was to recreate the church *in its form* from the ground up. Instead, most of the early Reformers borrowed the style, feel, rituals, and types of liturgies of Roman Catholicism. The Reformers didn't finish the application of their new theology to the concrete form of the church. This is why people often claim that such-and-such movement or theologian's ideas "completed" the Reformation.

Like post-Reformation churches, virtual churches haven't completely recreated worship for the virtual world; most are still relying on forms of worship that represent their traditions in the real world. In Second Life, the Anglican Cathedral chose a cathedral rather than a tree house, a moonbase, or an aquarium for their meeting place because they felt that at this early stage in the process, people need to see an architecture they recognize as church.[1] Internet campuses, perhaps by their very nature, tend to stick even closer to the form of worship practiced by the mother church. Overall, it can be a good thing for most virtual churches to begin with their tradition. The negative, though, is that if over the long term, virtual churches only replicate real-world forms — and think and visualize in real-world terms — they will never grasp the potential of being the church in the virtual world.[2]

Everyone wants to claim that their church, their movement, or their ecclesiology is "closest" or a "return" to the early church. Frankly, I get sick and tired of that argument. I don't care how many books are published each year that claim such-and-such movement is the real Acts 2 way; they're all disingenuous. Why can't we accept the fact that we will never again be just like the early church? That no one will ever again be swallowed by a fish for three days and regurgitated to call Nineveh to repentance?[3] That we don't need to be a carbon copy of what we guess the earliest church was really like to be faithful to God's call? That we should do the best we can today to reach today's generation in the way that God has prepared for today?

What makes the church, the church — rather than a shrine, temple, mosque, or geodesic dome — is its universality, its adaptability. The church is the church because God created it to be not an organization built on culture or ideology but an organism made alive by the Spirit of God interacting with people. All things being equal, the church can exist anywhere that people can exist, but the same may not be true for many world religions. Let me say it another way: many other non-Christian religions have rituals or superstitions that don't appear to be easily adaptable to life in the virtual world because they are products of real-world geography, physics, rituals, or forms.[4] In contrast, God's church and his kingdom are not products of the "real world" (John 18:36). This is the reason why a virtual church is and can be a real, valid church of Christ: God is not constrained to any human definition of the real world or to any physical form of the church (John 4:24).

John Calvin explains this well, and without the encumbrance or bias of a modern worldview: God's kingdom "is neither bounded by location in space nor circumscribed by any limits. Thus Christ is not prevented from exerting his power wherever he pleases, in heaven and on earth. He shows his presence in power and strength, is always among his own people, and breathes his life upon them, and lives in them, sustaining them, strengthening, quickening, keeping them unharmed, as if he were present in the body."[5] God transcends any notion of real world we may conjure up — or any form or ritual of the church.

Virtual churches have a real opportunity to be the renewed church in perhaps the largest mission field in existence, and to reach into many hard to reach parts of the real world. However, they will not do this well simply by appropriating real-world church forms and adapting them for use in the virtual world; they must create new forms of worship — many of which would be difficult or impossible in the real world — that will harness the connective and equipping power of the virtual world, all the while keeping the focus on God's glory rather than on technology's wonders.

Beta Worship

A beta version of new software or a new gadget is the not-ready-for-prime-time version; it's the version with which early adopters get to play around and on which the creators and play testers get to look for bugs and try out new ideas. Right now, most virtual churches and internet campuses seem to be in the beta phase; they're trying out new forms of worship to see what will work best to be the church in the virtual world. It's a good thing, but what the world needs as soon as possible are more releasable versions, not beta versions. But while we're in the beta stage, let's raise some important questions.

How should the proclamation of the Word work in the virtual world? Most Christians would agree that the preaching and teaching aspect of the church is paramount in importance (Acts 2:42). Right now, it seems that most virtual churches favor very short messages. When I ask virtual-church pastors, the reasons they give for this are (a) technological limitations and (b) the attention spans of virtual churchgoers. While brief teaching times may be a necessity at the beta stage while we wait for the technology to catch up with the vision, they could present a real weakness if it stays this way in the future. Should virtual-church proclamation be driven by the attention spans of multitasking computer users? While longer is not necessarily better, there is evidence that the nature of virtual worlds tends to encourage informational blurbs rather than the real communication and dialog necessary for the growth and discipleship of spiritually healthy people.[6] The goal for virtual churches must be to have healthy churches, not weak churches.

If lengthy sermons are out (for the time being at least), then virtual churches will have to envision a new way to encourage spiritual growth through proclamation. Can virtual churches present multiple minimessages in one extended worship time, allowing people to come in and out as time permits? Can the decentralized nature of the medium allow for a shorter message with immediate small-group breakouts in the same service, which people would participate in via avatar? Can virtual churches leverage technology to make the entire message participatory (real-time polling, IM shoutouts, quotable tickers), allowing greater length and greater depth? It appears that the idea that "everyone participates" is a key to virtual worlds, and there are ways that we can reformulate the message to take advantage of people's desire to participate.

Along the same lines, it seems likely the virtual world can let us reimagine our use of testimonies in worship. Right now, most real-world churches tend to use written testimonies on handouts and websites, though they use "live" testimonies in their services. We all know live ones are more powerful than written ones, even though they are usually prepared in advance (because of the nervousness of the speaker and related factors). Most pastors recognize that some of the greatest testimonies are those given in the moment, in the rough, from the heart. For the most part, it is hard for real-world churches to take advantage of spontaneous testimonies (unless they have spontaneous services), but virtual churches can pretty easily implement such testimonies due to the peer-to-peer nature of computer-mediated communication. Testimonies can be posted on the fly, even in the midst of worship or proclamation. Already, many virtual churches that use the internet-campus approach use interactive forums during worship services. The nature of the virtual medium encourages interactivity more than real-world churches probably could imagine (especially in light of the fear of public speaking). Even though virtual testimonies are very public, there's no fear factor.[7]

Many virtual churches seem to lack the depth of praise that can occur in churches in the real world. Mostly because of the limitations of technology or the infrastructure of a virtual church, many virtual churches seem to struggle with praise times in their current beta versions. Understandably, they don't want to make the technological faux pas of including anything that sounds like a midi-based cyber-hymnal. There is also the real fear that it will feel weird for people to sing along to a computer screen. I believe this is somewhat cultural and will change over time; for example, every time I attend some megachurch conference simulcast at an extension center, some people sing during the worship as if it were live, and some don't sing at all. Over the years, I have noticed more people taking part. What will really make the difference is when the technology is fast enough that you can hear other people singing in the background (a feedback loop), just like in the real world.

In contrast to this is LifeChurch.tv, which, as with other churches following the internet-campus approach, uses full broadcast-quality praise worship in their virtual-world venues. What makes their method different is that they offer several different formats for worship. At the time I visited their internet campus, they had two options. Maybe virtual churches will one day even have multiple styles — say alternative rock and R&B — but I look forward to when German nümetal and polka praise are possibilities. The Abba Father Inter-Continental Internet Church does the same thing, liturgically speaking, offering text-based worship services somewhat tailored to hundreds of different people groups. Still, it does raise the question, Is there a better approach to virtual-church praise than dialing in one of several optional channels with streaming praise media? What new forms of praise will virtual churches generate? Since worship is an action — showing worth to a holy God — not just listening to cool music, the answer would seem to be that virtual churches must look to a new form of praise — something musical, lively, attractive, but somehow more "wiki, wiki," more participatory.

What types of spiritual disciplines will flourish in virtual churches? Since everyone agrees that prayer has no geographical or spatial requirements, it seems to be an obvious strength of virtual churches (1 Tim. 2:8). In the years since its creation, i-church has found prayer to be a central part of its virtual worship.[8] Prayer in the virtual world has proven to be extremely meaningful for a variety of reasons, but one of the most interesting reasons is that the virtual world innately encourages the best of individual and intercessory prayer practices. When a virtual worshiper wants to make a prayer request, computer-mediated communication amplifies the reach of the prayer, sending it to other worshipers in real time, much as a real-world "prayer chain" might, just with more immediate and longer-lasting consequences. To see how this works, we can compare it to real-world practices; small-group prayer times often feel more personal and far more powerful than reading large prayer lists in the church bulletin or other less intimate situations. As a pastor, I often wonder how many of my people pray for these "impersonal" types of prayer requests, whereas if virtual worshipers get even a couple of hits to their prayer requests, it feels as intimate as small-group time.[9] So we see that the virtual world has the power to magnify communication, but can it magnify the *power* (effectiveness) of prayer? Not from God's perspective, of course, but prayer can provide an indirect benefit for people too (John 11:41 – 43). It is quite possible that prayers in virtual places will be reprayed for days, weeks, or years to come — in this sense, quite a magnification over most real-world possibilities. For example, what if I put a tag on the bottom of my personal web page that reads, "Thanks for visiting! Please pray for my family before leaving!" This example may sound silly, but depending on the traffic to my website over the next forty or more years, my family could be lifted up in prayer quite a lot. The more prayer, the better (1 Thess. 5:17).

The spiritual discipline of prayer is a great example of some similarities between worship in the virtual world and worship in the real world. Virtual-church pastors can integrate spiritual disciplines that require a physical component, such as fasting, Bible study, solitude, and confession, into a virtual-world church just as easily as real-world church pastors can. For example, in the real world, we don't usually practice solitude during our Sunday worship services; it's something that people decide to do themselves in concert with their church. The same will be true in virtual churches. One spiritual practice that may be hurt by virtual churches is the practice of honoring the Sabbath. While I suspect that the decline in observing the Sabbath has more to do with culture than technology, it seems to me that virtual churches will have to work even harder than real-world churches to disciple their attendees in this area. It will be an even greater temptation on the part of virtual-church attendees to "squeeze in a virtual service" each week rather than set aside a time of concentrated devotion to God (Mark 2:27; Rom. 14:6).

During the last half of the twentieth century, many Western church leaders spent a great deal of time engaged in futile debates over music styles in worship services. Given the coming impact of virtual (and augmented) worlds, will the debates of the twenty-first century be over visual styles (as it was in the eighth and ninth centuries, for example)? As visual representation, photonic, and holographic technologies create augmented worship worlds for real-world churches, virtual churches could lead the way in inventing fresh visual styles for worship. Here I am speaking of far more than just video content (though that is a start). Each week, a virtual church could choose to worship in a different environment (catacombs for a series on faith, outer space for a series on evangelism) and enhance the proclamation of the Word through faith-empowering visual displays — the ultimate stained-glass experience. The virtual world has the ability not just to produce images but also to immerse worshipers and create discipleship opportunities in a visual expression of faith as if every worship experience were in the Sistine Chapel.[10] Churches with internet campuses tend to take a functional approach to virtual worship — a necessity, perhaps, today because of technological restraints, but something to be reconsidered as technology improves. Protestants such as myself may end up envious of

Enos Andel reflects on the power of visual worship at an Orthodox church in Second Life.

more visually oriented groups such as the Orthodox Church, who have greater experience in this area; for example, the Greek Orthodox Archdiocese of America has a virtual collection of real icons in 3D virtual space.[11] The visual possibilities for virtual churches are endless.

Reformatting Rituals

As virtual churches find their own voices for worship, one concern plagues their progress and their acceptance by many ordinary Christians: can or should a virtual church perform ordinances or sacraments in a virtual world? I believe this concern has become an unnecessary sticking point in the discussion of virtual churches, and unfortunately has become something of a rallying cry for those opposed to the idea of virtual churches as authentic expressions of church. We might expect Christians from denominations with so-called high or structured views of the sacraments (such as Roman Catholicism and Eastern Orthodoxy) to be hesitant to embrace Communion in virtual churches,[12] but even Christians coming from denominations with so-called low or relaxed views of the ordinances often raise this issue. When the subject of virtual churches comes up, the first question I am always asked is, Are virtual churches real? and the second always is, Well, how do they do Communion?

I believe there are several reasons why everyone interested in virtual churches is curious about the handling of the sacraments — beyond the basic issues of their importance in historic Christian faith, and not to mention the long-standing disagreements over their observance. For one, the ordinances are personal, very meaningful to all Christians; there is a much finer line between acceptability and sacrilege in sacramental practice than in other areas of church practice. Virtual-church pioneers must walk with caution as they begin to observe the ordinances in their internet campuses. For another, I believe the practice of the sacraments in virtual worlds will reveal a great deal about the sacraments themselves and their significance for the Christian faith. Without doubt, Christians' great reverence for the sacraments explains their keen interest in how virtual churches administer them.

So, can virtual churches observe real sacraments? Let's begin our discussion with Communion, and then we'll turn to baptism.[13]

Communion

At the outset, we must realize that in our discussion of Communion, we face an overwhelming dilemma: since the major Christian traditions have all wrangled over the meaning and practice of the Lord's Supper in the real world for millennia, it would be impossible for us to discuss the validity and practice of the Lord's Supper in the virtual world in a way that addresses every issue or makes every tradition happy. As a result, we'll just take into account the major issues on which most Christians, regardless of tradition, agree. Even worse, there is some confusion over what one means by virtual Communion, so we'll need to define that term too. Let's start with what we know about Communion.

Regardless of Jesus' public ministry practices or rumored table fellowships with his followers, the Lord's Supper was a special fellowship begun during Jesus' final supper near to or during the final Passover meal. The sharing of the bread and wine was not the main meal (Matt. 26:26; Acts 20:7), though it was not a stand-alone ritual either.[14] Jesus consecrated the bread and wine as a sign of the new covenant with God (Luke 22:19 – 20). From the very beginning, the Lord's Supper was an integral part of the early church (Acts 2:42, 46). Again, the description in Acts distinguishes the Lord's Supper from a simple communal meal (held by many house churches and Anabaptists),[15] but it doesn't in any way suggest it was a detached liturgical ritual (as practiced by most sacramental denominations).[16] As usual, the New Testament doesn't prescribe an exact ritual performance to follow,[17] though it does appear to outline parameters generally accepted by the early church (1 Cor. 11:23 – 29).[18]

One thing that is indisputable is that the Bible never puts forward any rules governing the physical or spatial requirements for the Lord's Supper (except for the broken bread and imbibed wine, of course). More specifically, the Bible never puts forward any rules that determine what makes Communion "real." Its singular concern seems to be the spiritual condition of the partakers. This is true of the writings of the early church fathers as well. As a result, many groups in church history have tried to fill in and codify the missing "requirements" themselves, which is always a recipe for disaster. But it is this very thing, this lack of objective rules or limits (as Calvin suggested about the nature of the church), that makes the Lord's Supper the remembrance of and thanksgiving for a sacrificial savior sent from a living and active God, rather than a ritual for a mute idol. In light of this, it seems that there is nothing inherently unbiblical about observing Communion in a virtual church, though there will be a great deal of discussion over the actual practice of Communion in the virtual world.

By my unofficial count, most virtual churches and internet campuses have chosen to abstain from celebrating the Lord's Supper in any regular fashion, often for fear of offending people who have different sacramental views.[19] In my opinion, this is a big mistake. If a virtual church is a real church, should it not celebrate the Lord's Supper in accordance with Christian tradition? Absolutely, it should. When a virtual church abstains from observing ordinances, it raises questions about its validity as a church.[20] Far more important, when a virtual church refrains from any practice of the Lord's Supper, it runs the risk of dishonoring Jesus' request and joining company with theologically suspect groups.[21] To move out of the beta phase of worship, virtual churches must address this deficiency and include Communion and other important faith practices; they need to share in the "one loaf" of the body of Christ (1 Cor. 10:17). How, then, can or should virtual churches practice virtual Communion?

As I mentioned, there isn't any standard definition of virtual Communion. One way we can eliminate confusion is to look at several methods that virtual churches can (and do) use to observe virtual Communion. To help our discussion, I have classified virtual-Communion practices into four main types, and I have created names for each method to make things easier. (There may be other methods or types of virtual Communion other than these four.) We can then discuss the merits and demerits of each style of virtual Communion.

The first approach some virtual churches take is *symbolic virtual Communion*. This is the observance of the Lord's Supper by reading about Communion and meditating on the symbol of the Lord's Supper, or an individual's isolated practice of the meal after reading from a website and meditating. We see this style most frequently at text-driven virtual churches that describe the Communion practice on their website, and then offer the reader the opportunity to either meditate on or administer Communion to themselves at their computer. The benefit of this approach is that it is relatively low-tech and oriented to the convenience of the individual. But there are several big negatives with this approach. First, it encourages the fabrication of imaginary communities; a person may go to a popular church website to celebrate Communion not realizing that they are the only one there at the time celebrating Communion.[22] Second, for those traditions that believe a priest or some other qualified person must administer Communion, this method of Communion won't seem to work.[23] Third, there is the real danger that symbolic virtual Communion is too dissimilar from traditional Communion. For example, anytime I teach on fasting at church, people always ask me if they can fast from TV (or whatever) instead. The problem is that even though abstaining from watching TV (or whatever) can be a good thing, it's not really fasting.[24] Reading about, meditating on, or taking Communion individually may be acceptable as a type of personal worship, but it doesn't seem to fit any traditional description of Communion. I believe virtual churches should be wary of this approach.

A second approach to observing the Lord's Supper that we find in virtual worlds is *avatar-mediated virtual Communion*. This is the practice of administering the Lord's Supper through an avatar or other virtual medium to other avatars. For example, during a virtual worship service in a 3D virtual world, I instruct my avatar to eat a consecrated virtual loaf and drink from a consecrated virtual cup, without eating and drinking with my physical body. This practice is different from symbolic virtual Communion in that I am taking Communion through my avatar within a corporate gathering of the body of Christ (Acts 2). The benefit of this method is that anyone around the world can take part, without worrying about the elements or trying to find unleavened bread and wine or grape juice. Since I live in North America, it is hard to visualize a place in our world where that would be a benefit, though I have been in parts of Africa where there is cell-phone (and potentially web) service but no obvious access to the Communion elements. Another benefit would be that a qualified person could offer virtual Communion in avatar form. (There is a third benefit, but I'll address it in the section on avatar-mediated virtual baptism below.) The downside of avatar-mediated virtual Communion is similar to the downside of symbolic virtual Communion: this method of observing Communion seems too dissimilar to traditional descriptions of Communion.

Taken together, there is a substantial concern with both symbolic virtual Communion and avatar-mediated virtual Communion: the lack of physical elements consumed within community. The Bible and the testimony of the early church seem to make it pretty clear that Communion is a physical as well as a spiritual act (John 6:48–58; Luke 22:17). In 1 Corinthians 11, Paul addresses the struggle the church at Corinth was facing with Communion; the struggle was not over the theological meaning of Communion but over people trivializing the meal by eating too much, refusing to share with others, and similar issues related to the hearts of people demonstrated by their physical actions. Therefore, we should judge different attempts at virtual Communion primarily on the *communion* of the people, not the details of the administration. Whether in the real or the virtual world, no church is immune to these dangers.

Still, certain Christian traditions of the church in its middle and later history have especially emphasized the reality of the bread and the cup. Since symbolic virtual Communion and avatar-mediated Communion don't practice the consumption of physical elements in community, a virtual church that practices virtual Communion with these methods runs the risk of unintentionally trivializing the Lord's Supper — and overspiritualizing what was meant to be a simple celebration after a shared meal. Moreover, these approaches to virtual Communion confuse realities (natures and essences): virtual churches are real churches because they are real people meeting faithfully in synthetic space, but real people can't take Communion with synthetic elements. Real people, even those in synthetic space, should probably use real elements. If a virtual church selects either of these two models, it must find a way to avoid trivializing or overspiritualizing Communion in the hearts of its people.

A third approach to administering the Lord's Supper in virtual churches is *extensional virtual Communion*.[25] In this practice, a virtual church shares Communion together (telepresent in real time in synthetic space) using real elements that have been extended to members of the community in some manner by the pastor or priest. For example, I might log in to my regular internet campus, and when the pastor brings out the bread and the cup for the congregation during the live service, I use prepared bread and juice to observe Communion along with the rest of my virtual church (typing or speaking, "He did this for you," to others in the forum). In this example, I say "prepared" since different traditions will have different expectations for the elements. "Prepared" could mean the elements were prepared by the individual, were gathered by a regional layperson or deacon, or were consecrated in advance by a priest and shipped from the mother church. The benefits of this method are that people are taking Communion together in real community and that people are receiving real elements, regardless of whether they are worshiping in real or synthetic space.[26] Whatever the situation, a virtual churchgoer can take virtual Communion with physical and even consecrated elements during a live worship service in a local, virtual church.

If we look to church history, it affirms the benefits of extensional virtual Communion. The church has always made provision for those who are sick, shut in, or dying to receive Communion in their homes or places of convalescence. Both Justin Martyr, an early-second-century Christian apologist from Roman Syria, and Cyprian, Bishop of Carthage in the third century, validate this practice in the early church.[27] Both Cyprian and Tertullian report that people were even allowed to keep consecrated elements in their homes.[28] While the medieval period brought sharp changes to the administration of Communion (especially in the Roman Catholic Church, which was one issue that precipitated the Protestant Reformation), most Christian denominations have some office, benediction, or blessing for Communion by extension. Even to this day, most Christian traditions have some provision for Communion by extension.[29]

Some will object that my analogy of the ancient practice of Communion by extension (reserved sacrament) for the sick is an unfair comparison, since this type of Communion is a special act of grace for people with real needs, whereas virtual Communion is for generally healthy people who prefer to worship in front of their computers for whatever reason. Either way, it doesn't matter; the church at large created Communion by extension (and other similar sacramental derivations) to extend Communion to the church as far and as wide as possible. This example works because church tradition encourages churches and their leaders to advocate the sacraments for people, as long as there's true repentance and redemption. In fact, any time the church has gone down the road of limiting Communion for people, such as at the fifteenth-century Council of Constance — a reprehensible and disastrous moment for the church at large — it has proven to be against the interests of Christ and his kingdom.[30]

Still, there are some negatives to extensional virtual Communion. As with the other forms of virtual Communion, there remains some danger of trivialization. Another negative is that many traditions will be uncomfortable with people preparing their own elements,[31] and some will find it a hassle (or impossible) to prepare elements to ship to parishioners around the world for a virtual Communion service. (What do you do if FedEx is late with the elements?) Still another issue is the elements used: one virtual church encouraged their people to substitute other elements for the bread and the cup. It will be problematic in most church traditions if people were to choose Fig Newtons and Coca-Cola to observe the Lord's Supper at virtual churches.

A fourth approach to observing the Lord's Supper in virtual churches is *outsourced virtual Communion*. This method of virtual Communion occurs when a virtual church establishes contact with real-world churches to set up special situations in which their virtual churchgoers can take the Lord's Supper in a real-world church. This method might work best for virtual churches originating from traditions with so-called higher views of Communion. The benefit of this approach to virtual Communion is that it eliminates the virtual aspect of Communion; the person attends church in the virtual world but takes Communion in the real world. Even with this approach, there are quite a few negatives. First, there is the complication of connecting virtual churchgoers with real-world churches, especially if virtual churches have a worldwide reach (as they all seem to have). What if the virtual churchgoer lives where there is no church of the same denomination as the virtual church? Or where there are very few churches to begin with? Or where the nearest churches won't offer Communion to outsiders? Second, there is the whole issue of outsourcing Communion. While we'll take this up in more detail when we discuss baptism, it seems unhealthy, or worse, to outsource Communion to another faith service provider rather than observing it as a community as intended; it seems to destroy the whole idea of communion.

In the end, virtual churches must no longer withhold the bread and the cup from their people if they want to move out of the beta phase and claim to be true expressions of the church. They must work out the details, satisfy their traditions' requirements, and bless their people with the Lord's Supper. Modern-day versions of the Lord's Supper that seem normal to us — whether administered communally in precious chalices with opaque wafers, or in little plastic cups with bland breadlike squares — would appear strange indeed to early Christians. Whether we want to admit it or not, the modern church in every form and of every type has adapted the Lord's Supper to modern conventions. Even though virtual Communion will seem strange to many today, we must continue to adapt our expressions of the church and its ordinances for every circumstance in light of our divine mandate (Matt. 28:18 – 20). On the issue of Communion, virtual churches should not fear people's opinions or church traditions but should fear dishonoring Jesus' request: "Do this to remember me" (Luke 22:19).

Baptism

What about baptism? How should virtual churches handle baptizing new believers? And what about virtual infant baptism?

As with Communion, baptism is a vital ordinance in which the covenant people of God participate. And as with Communion, virtual churches must wrestle with how they will perform baptism for their new members. Still, there are some fundamental differences between the Lord's Supper and baptism that affect our discussion. For one, while both Communion and baptism appear to require physical elements, the elements in Communion are much more specific than the elements in baptism. (Any type of water anywhere will do for most traditions.) For another, baptism, more so than Communion, necessitates that another (and qualified) person be present to perform the ordinance. Finally, baptism occurs only once, whereas Communion is a regular practice for each believer. While some virtual churches have already performed virtual baptisms, most are hesitant to stick their toes in the water.

Baptism has a longer history than the Lord's Supper, though its origin is far murkier. We know that ancient Hebrew worship practices included ceremonial washing and ritual cleansing (Lev. 8:6; Num. 8:6 – 7). The idea of ritual cleansing was perhaps quite popular in the century or two before Jesus lived, as can be seen in the Dead Sea Scrolls (documents from a Jewish sect). In my experience, many churchgoers (and almost all nonchurchgoers) view baptism as some type of purification ritual ("purifying a person from their sins"). However, there are significant problems when we liken baptism to cleansing. The best way to briefly explain the turn from the use of water as an act of habitual cleansing to its being a symbol of the believer's death and initiation into God's covenant household is Ezekiel 36:25 – 26: "I will sprinkle clean water on you, and you will be clean; I will cleanse you from all your impurities and from all your idols. I will give you a new heart and put a new spirit in you."[32] This prophetic passage speaks in the language of cleansing to express a promise from God for a singular redemptive act indicated by baptism. This idea is fulfilled in the New Testament when we see John the Baptist practice a baptism of repentance (Matt. 3:5 – 6; Acts 19:4) and when Paul explains baptism as death to a person's old ways leading to covenant union with Jesus (Rom. 6:3 – 8). Thus, Christian baptism stems not from religious cleansing but from an expression of repentance in an act of identifying ourselves with Christ's salvific death and with his community (1 Peter 3:21).[33]

What else do we know about baptism? First, we know that the confession of sins (repentance) is a precondition of baptism (Matt. 3:6; Acts 2:38).[34] Second, we know it is tied very closely to, and is representative of, salvation (Mark 16:16; 1 Peter 3:21). Third, we know that baptism implies the union of the believer with Christ — and therefore the church — and does not allow for baptism outside of community.[35] Fourth, we expect a church to carry out baptism (explicitly, or at minimum implicitly) in the name of the Father, Son, and Spirit (Matt. 28:19). Fifth, we know that baptism in the Bible was a real, not symbolic, event that used real water. While the Bible doesn't go into many details about how to baptize, there are clear instances when the baptizer fully dunked the baptizee into water (Matt. 3:16; Acts 8:38 – 39).

Very similar to the case with Communion, the Bible never sets any rules outlining the physical or spatial requirements for baptism (not counting water), or any guidelines as to what makes baptism "real" (save perhaps confession as a precondition, and the invocation of the Father, Son, and Spirit as the seal); the Bible is far more interested in highlighting the spiritual aspects of baptism and its significance for believers. One very early document of the early church is the *Didache*, also known as *The Teaching of the Twelve Apostles*. While scholars debate its exact provenance,[36] it is definitely the earliest Christian discussion on the details of baptism outside of the Bible. The *Didache* explains that a church should baptize a candidate in the name of the Father, Son, and Holy Spirit, and lists several different acceptable modes of performing baptism.[37] Tertullian, an early church father, also insisted that the exact mode of baptism didn't much matter.[38] While there is considerable textual, historical, and archaeological evidence that baptism by immersion was the method practiced most in the early church, it would be wrong to suggest that other methods are categorically invalid.

Therefore, just as with Communion, there doesn't appear to be any inherent biblical reason not to practice virtual baptism. Because baptism is absolutely essential for the church and its people, virtual churches must not abstain from practicing baptism or withhold it from its members. The problem remains the same as with virtual Communion: what do virtual churches mean when they speak of virtual baptism? Similar to the case with Communion, there are at least four ways that virtual churches can (and do) practice virtual baptism. (Though there are some issues that separate them from the four types of virtual Communion we discussed.) So we ask, How can or should virtual churches practice virtual baptism?

The first approach some virtual churches take is *symbolic virtual baptism*. This is the practice of baptism by reading about baptism and meditating on the symbol of baptism. Like symbolic virtual Communion, the weaknesses of symbolic virtual baptism are that it ignores the physical importance of water burial, possibly encourages imaginary communities, and introduces the possibility of self-baptism. Since water is everywhere, there doesn't appear to be any credible benefit to symbolic virtual baptism.

A second approach to baptism that we find in virtual worlds is *avatar-mediated virtual baptism*. This is the practice of an avatar (church leader) baptizing another avatar (baptismal candidate) in a virtual medium. For example, a virtual-church pastor in an avatar-based virtual world such as Second Life meets the convert at a synthetic body of water and immerses the convert in the name of the Father, Son, and Holy Spirit. The church could invite all of its members to witness the virtual baptism in avatar form. Besides the benefits of baptizing in the context of a real, telepresent community, and of the baptism potentially being administered by a qualified priest or pastor, there is the benefit of being able to baptize a person regardless of their real-world situation. Unlike the elements of avatar-mediated virtual Communion, water can be found everywhere, but one of the real-world issues most typified with baptism is the death of the convert to the old system (and culture) of life and the entrance into the new family of God. In most of North America, we take baptism for granted, but in many parts of the world, real-world baptism can be a dangerous enterprise. In predominantly Muslim countries in the Middle East, a convert to Christianity often faces persecution or death for public conversion to Christianity. Converts from Islam "don't want to avoid baptism," explain missionaries Mike and Sally Williams, "but not all pastors [of Christian churches in the Middle East] have the courage to baptize" new believers.[39] In parts of the world like the Middle East, where internet evangelism is extremely effective, could avatar-mediated baptism at a virtual church be a credible solution to the dangers of real-world baptism — and open the door for more former Muslims to enter into real Christian community? While avatar-mediated baptism still carries the strong downside of being waterless, it's potential in hostile parts of our real world probably deserves serious consideration and further investigation.

A third method of virtual baptism is *extensional virtual baptism*. In this type of virtual baptism, a virtual church baptizes a new believer using real water but through a telepresent experience with a qualified pastor or priest. The internet campus at Flamingo Road Church has baptized converts in this manner. In one recent baptism, the candidate was baptized by telepresent Senior Pastor Troy Gramling and Internet Campus Pastor Brian Vasil, assisted by a physically present Christian friend of the candidate, with both parties able to hear and see each other through webcam. The positive of extensional virtual baptism is that people are baptized in real, not synthetic, water and within a real, telepresent community. One negative of this approach is that it won't work for people who live in areas with computer access but without many Christians (especially Christians willing to baptize other Christians). Other negatives are that some traditions may not recognize the validity of an unqualified "helper" to assist in the baptism, and that it may seem like self-baptism (though in the case of Flamingo Road, clearly it is not). Still, taken at face value, extensional virtual baptism seems a credible possibility.

A fourth approach to baptism in virtual churches is *outsourced virtual baptism*.[40] In this method, a virtual church contacts a real-world church to set up a special baptismal service for their candidate in the real-world church. The benefit of this approach is that a candidate can be baptized in the real world in a real-world church context. In light of the fact that baptism is a one-time event, this approach will seem to many people to be the best approach — including several virtual-church pastors I interviewed. At the same time, there is a serious downside. Since most Christian traditions view baptism as the beginning of new community for the new believer, how can virtual churches be real, authentic Christ communities if they can't even perform the basic ordinance of community formation? This is the issue that Flamingo Road Internet Campus struggled with. Brian Vasil explains that in the case of their first virtual baptism, the person was such a regular, committed member of the virtual church, "we thought we would be selling out our own [church] by not figuring out a way to baptize [the person]," even if it meant a virtual baptism.[41]

Before we leave the subject of virtual baptism, we must at least raise the question, What about virtual infant baptism? Let me say up front that I am not part of a tradition that practices infant baptism, and so I will speak as an outsider. While I have not heard of a virtual church that has performed virtual infant baptism, it seems quite likely — at least from a theological perspective — that virtual infant baptism may be less controversial in some ways than adult believer's baptism. For example, while the positives and negatives of symbolic virtual baptism remain unchanged in the case of infant baptism, the other three types of virtual baptism lose some of their negatives, since infant baptism is generally seen as either a response to God's call to baptize people or the general introduction of the infant into the larger covenant family of God. Nevertheless, some Christians will ask, If virtual churches baptize babies through virtual baptism, won't that contribute to more adolescents and young adults walking away from the church? The problem with this argument, I believe, is that it implies that virtual infant baptism is less real than real-world infant baptism, an argument that doesn't hold water from a biblical or theological perspective (especially for extensional or outsourced virtual infant baptism).

Decompartmentalizing the Church

I began this chapter with the story of prayer in Kenya, a story that reveals that what we think is normative practice in the church rests largely on our cultural milieu and place in history than on some pure biblical form. Even deeply spiritual practices such as the Lord's Supper and baptism rely on modern conventions and forms to express ancient truths. It is difficult, and for many people is a terribly grating feeling, to have to reformulate these practices in a new way for a new time for a new people, but we must, if we wish to remain faithful to our covenant with God to be the church.

In each of these transitions, there are trade-offs. Are there negatives to administering virtual Communion? You bet. There are negatives with ritualistic, stylized, performance Communions; there are negatives with shrink-wrapped, stadium-seat Communions; there are negatives with inward-looking, chaste, commune Communions. So we should not be surprised that there are negatives whenever we take part in ancient Christian practices, whether in the modern real world or in the virtual world. Many Christians will ask, Isn't there a real loss from not being able to gather physically and hand the cup and bread to other people in a particular, local church, speaking blessing into their lives and saying, "He did this for you"? Of course there is. At the same time, I hear the powerful testimonies coming out of virtual churches, and it makes me wonder: is the loss of physical touch in Christian practice somehow counterbalanced by the connective strengths of computer-mediated communication? In real-world churches, don't many Christians also feel a loss during Communion because of performance, size, or domestication of the practice? And in some cases, isn't one Christian's loss another Christian's gain? To say it another way, some Christians lament the loss of the smells and bells while others gain the freedom to worship in a more relaxed manner. While there is the obvious loss of physical touch in virtual Christian practices, there are likely to be gains for many Christians. One gain is that virtual sacraments — especially Communion — free the worshiper from the peer pressure inherent in real-world contexts in order to better examine themselves before participating (or even choosing not to participate).[42] In the case of Communion, another possibility is that virtual Communion recasts the remembrance — itself a virtual act — and engrosses the partaker in a way that is beyond the capacity of most modern worship forms.[43] Could virtual sacraments reinvigorate the use of sacraments in real-world churches?[44]

We can see the potential of virtual Communion only if we are willing to decompartmentalize the church — to accept that a local church is not the end all and be all of the kingdom of God but is just one part of the larger body. We may hope these different parts of the body will work together. Just because a virtual church meets regularly in a virtual world doesn't mean it has to do *everything* in a virtual world. The real-world church I pastor meets in a bricks-and-mortar building, but praise God it doesn't mean we have to do *everything* in that building. Today, and into the future, the people of God will inhabit the real world, virtual worlds, and augmented worlds, and there will be churches existing in each of the three — and most will adapt parts of their churches to all three. However, the fluid nature of worlds, and the growing desire to adapt and customize resources on the level of the local church, will raise significant questions about ecclesiastical authority and the decentralization of worship, faith, and practice.

VIRTUAL WEDDINGS AND FUNERALS

Real-world churches regularly hold worship services that include special practices such as Communion, baptism, and experiences tied to the various spiritual disciplines, but there are other aspects of church life and Christian worship — specifically, performing marriages and funerals. How will virtual churches deal with weddings and funerals?

Actually, virtual weddings are nothing new. The first virtual wedding took place in 1996, and many more have taken place in the virtual world since that time.[a] Since the bride, groom, and pastor can all be telepresent in the same synthetic space, a wedding is quite doable (and probably very affordable) in the virtual world.[b] Virtual churches could perform virtual weddings for couples who are temporarily separated by geography, though this raises the question of the wisdom of marrying two people who are not physically present together. Perhaps more realistically, pastors could perform virtual marriage counseling for couples who live apart geographically but are planning to marry.[c]

However, before virtual pastors start marrying people, there is a very significant legal problem they will need to address: jurisdiction. Countries, states, or regions often have different laws regarding weddings, and if the pastor resides in one country or state, and the bride and groom reside in a different country or state, the pastor might need the legal right to marry in both places. The same holds true if the bride and groom live in separate countries or states; they might need to fulfill the legal requirements for both jurisdictions.[d] Virtual weddings are no problem for virtual churches, as long as the bride and groom consult a qualified marriage licensing facilitator or agency in their state or country.

Funerals in the virtual world could be a very good idea in several ways, if handled properly. First, let's distinguish between the funeral service and the mortuary process. Since churches don't normally handle the mortuary process, a family wanting a virtual funeral would allow the funeral home to oversee the physical burial and graveside committal, but they could schedule a funeral service in the virtual world. A virtual funeral service does have several advantages. It is often difficult for people who live apart from the deceased to travel to a funeral; virtual funerals allow everyone to be present. Since the virtual world allows for customization, it is relatively easy to design a synthetic place with special meaning for the grieving family to hold the service; for example, if the deceased was a former naval officer, the family could hold the funeral on the deck of a virtual aircraft carrier. Obviously, the greatest negative of virtual funerals is the inability of people not physically present to express sympathy to the bereaved through physical gestures such as hugs and holding hands. As technology improves, virtual funerals or memorial services may become quite common.

----

a.   Simon Jenkins, "Rituals and Pixels: Experiments in Online Church," *Online-Heidelberg Journal of Religions on the Internet* 3:1 (2008): 99.
b.   Virtual weddings would be very inexpensive compared with real-world weddings!
c.   This could have been useful for my wife and me prior to our marriage, as we lived in different geographical areas for most of our dating period.

d. In the United States, several states, such as New York, have had a great deal of problems with jurisdiction, in most cases involving brides and grooms who choose to be married by friends who were ordained on the internet (especially those ordained as Jedi, swamis, gurus, or other religious groups with no legal standing). In New York, this is against state law, even though most of these people think they are legally married; see Devan Sipher, "Great Wedding! But Was It Legal?" *New York Times*, August 5, 2007.

chapter 6

Almighty Mod

"So who's in charge of this church, anyway?"

I could hear the words coming out of his mouth, but I needed to choose my words carefully before I answered him. To a certain degree, I punted the question.

"Well, Cameron, the pastoral staff and I handle most of the day-to-day decisions at BVC, but the advisory board makes all of the major decisions that don't need a congregational vote."

Cameron thought about my answer for about four seconds.

"How do I get on this advisory board?"

Such was one of my first conversations with a ministry leader after I had just taken the position as lead pastor at Berryessa Valley Church. Cameron had been in the church for several years, and while he was open to some changes, like most average churchgoers he was most interested in changes with which he was most comfortable. Cameron was a faithful follower of Jesus, but he spent the first several months of my pastorate raising questions about my authority to make changes at BVC.[1]

If you're a pastor, you've had this happen to you countless times, and the more churches you've pastored, the more you've encountered it. Just because a group of people gathers in an orderly fashion to worship God each week doesn't mean that the organization and administration of the church proceed in an orderly fashion. Unfortunately, if you want to see a real-life fight club, all you have to do is go to a church's business meeting.

What complicates these issues, and what makes people like Cameron ask leading questions, is that authority in the average church can reside in both traditional and nontraditional areas. Sure, we know who the pastor is, and some churches have elders, but church authority is way more tricky than this. As many average churchgoers have found out the hard way, churches really tend to struggle with this issue. Navigating church teams, boards, or committees is like trying to pick your way through a minefield.

Churches, as organizations, are also notorious for having entrenched power brokers. When a new young pastor fresh from seminary mentions to his new church family that he would like to see the church become more modern, why does everyone look at the blue-haired matriarch of the church to see what she will say? Authority in churches seems to come from strange places. In two churches in which I ministered, it was the janitor. The *janitor* was the final arbiter of what ministries could go where and when and how. If the janitor didn't approve, it didn't happen, at least not without a fight. In another church, several of the elders' wives were self-appointed rulers of their own little fiefdoms in the church. Average churchgoers at that church didn't realize that there were ministries where their own pastors feared to tread.

At the beginning of the twenty-first century, virtual churches face an issue that will define their ministries for generations — the issue of authority. The struggle for authority in the church has a long history, and it also plagues areas of the real world that have become newly virtual — from financial investments to scientific research to politics. We can find a great example of the virtual world's power to alter authority structures in the world of journalism — with the rise of the political blogosphere. Twenty years ago, no one could have imagined that hoity-toity news organizations such as the *New York Times* and CBS News would one day possess newsrooms that often are reactive instead of active, largely driven in their headline selection by the whims of a few maverick bloggers (such as the *Drudge Report* or the *Daily Kos*), or that internet-based news-opinion partisans would become the political power brokers in a US presidential election. What would happen if suddenly the voice of the church at large came not from among skilled denominational leaders or erudite theologians or even popular megachurch pastors but from among underground virtual churches led by nontraditional leaders or decentralized social groups emboldened by the power of computer-mediated communication? Will future virtual-world bishops be ideological mavericks, balanced pastors, or sheep bots bred in traditional denominational hierarchies? Or none of the above?

How should virtual churches relate to traditional authority? Can virtual churches harness the power of decentralization without further fracturing Christianity?

We all recognize that there is a "radical reformation" of sorts occurring within the Christian faith in virtual worlds. It's not just the endless blogs about the theological significance of that philosophical muddle of a movie trilogy starring Keanu Reeves a few years back; it's the fact that the virtual world gives anyone the means not only to discuss theology but to start their own virtual church. While it always has been possible for anyone to start their own church in the real world, the virtual world levels the playing field more than any event in recorded history. Come to think of it, there are already lots of churches in the virtual world. What do we know about them? Do we know who is behind them? Their leadership? Their authority? Their theology?[2] Sometimes we want to ask these questions of real-world church plants as well, but these issues seem to take on a new importance in the virtual world. We are tempted to ask related questions: Is the website or virtual-church moderator also the pastor or priest, or does someone else fill that role? How are any of these virtual-church leaders, whom we meet only as avatars, accountable to anyone?[3] Should they be?

An Open-Source Church

Even though we talk of the virtual world as an enlightened place that encourages progress and free thought, an intellectual war has been raging in this world since its inception. The combatants? Those people with power, and those people who feel that power should be redistributed, intellectual rights free for anyone to use, and digital property tweakable during personal use.[4] Another good example is the numerous skirmishes that have occurred in the last twenty years between Microsoft and computer users who want a computer with an operating system without all the things that Microsoft deems an operating system should be. They don't want Microsoft to decide what browser they can use; they want to decide. In classic guerrilla style, some of these users even created their own free, open-source operating system, Linux. It's open-source because users have access to the code and are free to tinker with it. It's an operating system created by the people for the people.

The genius behind virtual worlds such as Second Life is that they are largely open-source; users can create nearly anything they can imagine. Not only can they create it, they often own the digital rights to their creation. A church located in the clouds? Easy. A church with an interior design that changes color with the mood of the message, worship, or people? Very doable. A missile-command church that launches millions of avatar-seeking, gospel-tract ICBMs every day at every Second Life resident? No problem — at least until people complain, and then Second Life moderators have the power and authority to zap your church (and your rights) out of existence in the blink of an eye.[5] In the virtual world, they're the almighty mod.[6]

Inevitably, this war spilled over into the virtual-church world. The good news for the church at large is that, so far, there have been only a few isolated battles. One reason for this is that different sections of the church at large have different intentions when approaching the virtual world: there are quite a few churches and denominations that are choosing not to get involved in the virtual world at all; there are some theologians and church leaders who condemn the virtual world; there are some leaders from established churches and denominations who want to plant virtual churches entrenched in the stylistics of their real-world traditions; there are some virtual pastors who believe that virtual churches will finally fulfill the Great Commission (Matt. 28:18 – 20); and then there are the Christian free-thinkers who see the virtual world as a way to decentralize the church through their own brand of Christianity; and that's just to name a few. It's not that these perspectives don't exist in the real world when we discuss real-world churches; it's that the virtual world is changing the game for the church, and therefore we should expect an even more vigorous, many-sided, and complex debate to come.[7]

Let's look at an example of how the virtual world changes the authority game. In the real world, if a disgruntled Presbyterian elder decides, for whatever reason, enough's enough with old First Presbyterian Church, it is possible, but not easy, for the elder to leave and start an alternative Second Presbyterian down the street — the elder would face significant problems with finances, membership, synod approval, reputation, and much more. However, it is quite easy (and quick) for the elder to create Second Presbyterian Church of Second Life, appoint himself as its pastor, and invite a bunch of disaffected friends (not to mention people from around the world) to become members — finances, synod approval, and reputation would not be issues. People who visit the church, seeing the name and the well-designed virtual building, might be persuaded to join in fellowship. But what authority guides the start of this church? And is this church a legitimate expression of church? In the past, creating a new church by splitting from a larger Christian tradition typically required hard to acquire resources like financing, personal charisma, a provocative message, and great determination. In the virtual world, all that is required are a few pennies and the effort to learn the technology. A church can be created on a whim.

These possibilities trouble many well-meaning, traditional church leaders while at the same time excite many nontraditional Christians who feel that the establishment is part of the problem with church in the first place. As a result, at times the former is hesitant to engage the virtual world, even while the latter sees the virtual world as the great equalizer, since it allows for new approaches to worship and theology unfettered by traditional authority. To many nontraditional Christians, the virtual world is the New World, and they want to leave Old European authority structures behind. In the example of the disgruntled elder, the great megaphone of the virtual world presents a huge temptation simply to bypass the formal hierarchies and create a new church.[8] Is this a reformation? Or just an unhealthy way of dealing with problems?[9] Who decides?

This example is only a small piece of the larger puzzle of authority in the virtual world. The truth is it doesn't take a disgruntled elder to start a Presbyterian church; anyone from any religious background with any theology could go on Second Life and create Second Presbyterian.[10] If we fly around Second Life long enough on a Sunday, we'll see hundreds of churches to choose from dotting the virtual landscape. If we choose one at random, how do we know a real pastor leads the beautiful, inspiring church building we picked?[11] How do we know it's not led by a twelve-year-old kid who thought it would be a fun alternative to doing math homework?[12] (Is it inherently or biblically wrong to have a twelve-year-old as pastor?) Didn't we pick the church on aesthetics (it looks like a church) rather than on the authority of a church body or priest? Or the Bible?[13] Admittedly, we have these struggles in the real world. How *do* we know the new church down our real-world street is a legitimate church? Because of its name? Its building? Because the virtual world is a new phenomenon, we could argue that the average Christian will be better at seeing through church masquerades in the real world. Well, maybe. Maybe not.

This freedom works both ways. Since the inception of the virtual world, there's been a lot of flag waving by those who believe that it will usher in a new era for the church, that the church will throw off its hierarchical shackles and finally become all about people working together (as they believe the early church was, misunderstanding Acts 2). One example of this belief is the expectation that the church at large will evolve into a global, collaborative network of Christians on a mission rather than remaining as splintered groups of people who merely attend weekly ritual performances.[14] Certainly, virtual churches may help overturn traditional authority, as bloggers have done to CBS News, but won't this actually lessen the authority and legitimacy of all churches? Don't we have enough problems with x denominations or groups as it is, that we need x^n? The experimental nature of the virtual world has attracted many Christians who, at best, stand in variance to traditional Christianity or who, at worst, have a big axe to grind with traditional church or who advocate quasi-orthodox ideologies, or both.[15] These people may be well intentioned, but what authority or qualifications do they have to plant healthy virtual churches or internet campuses? Are these kinds of people really the best the church at large can get to engage the virtual world? Won't we lose something big if we jettison all tradition, hierarchy, and authority to create a global virtual commune of Christians?

Orphaned Sims

As virtual churches find their foothold in the church at large, there is a danger that the unrivaled power of computer-mediated communication and global telepresence will encourage virtual churches to act as if they are spiritual orphans, forgetting that they have close siblings in the multitude of real-world churches. They may choose to act like orphans to avoid debates over tradition, to escape real-world authority structures, or just to differentiate themselves from other churches, whether in the real world or the virtual world. Though I am an advocate of the Free Church model, this doesn't mean that I believe that individual churches should be isolated without accountability. Based on Paul's writings, I'm not sure that unconnected churches are biblical (1 Cor. 12:12). Regardless of our church backgrounds, we all should be able to agree with Paul Minear: "The New Testament offers no definition of the church per se as a separate or autonomous entity."[16] Churches with orthodox theologies and practices must not just work together; they must be different parts of the *same* body.

Revisiting the story of the disgruntled elder, let's assume that the elder decides to start Second Presbyterian in the real world, and that the Presbyterian powers that be don't come and remove the word *Presbyterian* from the new church's street sign. The elder — now pastor — decides that each Sunday service will be radically different from First Presbyterian; Second Presbyterian will not have a sermon but instead will allow everyone to speak, teach, prophesy, or say anything on his or her mind. There will be no elders or leaders; everyone will be equal. They will consider no creed or council to be normative. Does this elder have the authority to start Second Presbyterian Church in the real world? How about in the virtual world? Is the real-world Second Presbyterian a legitimate church? If Second Presbyterian buys First Baptist's building, is it now a legitimate church? In my understanding of ecclesiology, Second Presbyterian seems to be on shaky ground, with regard to both authority and legitimacy. While I can't judge the hearts of the elder or the people who join him, the purpose for Second Presbyterian seems spurious. I wouldn't recommend that people join this church, for several reasons. No matter how cut and dried our own ecclesiology is, these questions hit at the core of how a church becomes a church. Since this is so difficult to come to terms with in the real world, we can expect it to be even more difficult in the virtual world.

Let's switch from a hypothetical situation to a true story. When I was starting in ministry, I knew a rather unpleasant fellow who styled himself as a church planter and an evangelist, and even though the immediate area around where he lived had tons of seemingly healthy, legitimate churches, he decided to plant his own church (Silverlake Church). He canvassed neighborhoods and convinced about fifty people to come to his opening service; he even posted ads to get some future pastors to serve on staff with him *pro bono*. He launched Silverlake, and to be fair, his theology was largely within orthodoxy and the worship services were probably fine.[17] About eight months into the endeavor, the church had grown to eighty (this was in the Bible Belt) and was having a hard time finding a place to meet. Finding the increased ministry workload a burden, the fellow just announced one Sunday that that Sunday was his last — the church was on its own. He quit and walked away. If he felt any remorse, I never saw it. It seemed to be play church to him. It made me furious. Here was a pastor who had spiritually abandoned (and hurt) eighty

These two words (*authority* and *legitimacy*) open up a huge can of worms in any discussion of the church. On the one hand, Second Presbyterian may not have the authority to start a *Presbyterian* church from the human side of things (for example, synodal approval), but they might claim their freedom in Christ and start their church by the spiritual authority granted to all believers. Based on biblical and early-church data, I tend to think Westerners (at times) overstate this as a "right," as a way to do what we want to do, without working through the authority issue and receiving a blessing from the larger body (cf. Ignatius, *Letter to the Smyrnaeans* 9; Ignatius, *Letter to Polycarp* 6). Second Presbyterian appears to lack legitimacy for a couple of reasons. *Legitimate* means (a) legal and (b) "being exactly as purposed: neither spurious nor false" (*Merriam-Webster's Collegiate Dictionary*, 11th ed. [Springfield, Mass.: Merriam-Webster, 2003]). If a disgruntled elder starts a new church and rejects much of the practices and beliefs of his old church, is the new church spurious? It would seem so, but in the end only God knows.

people, as well as their larger community. Did these people find new churches? Some did, some didn't.

Did Silverlake, a real-world church, have the authority to be a church? If so, then what is the difference between this guy starting Silverlake in the real world, the disgruntled elder starting Second Presbyterian in either the real or the virtual world, and a twelve-year-old kid starting a church in the virtual world instead of doing math homework? All things being equal, there doesn't seem to be *any* discernable difference between these three examples of "church." Can we call Silverlake, this real-world play church, a legitimate church? Or was it a legitimate church, just one with a bad pastor? Couldn't we then call the twelve-year-old kid's virtual church a legitimate church with a bad (or at least immature) pastor?[18] See how easy it is for our Western worldview to kick in and influence us to think that somehow the real-world church is more legitimate, more "real," than the virtual-world church?

If we say Silverlake was a legitimate church with a bad pastor, why did it just close up shop as if it were a business or a club and everyone walk away? After all, when Church of Fools closed down, nobody wanted to walk away. Could a virtual-world church like Church of Fools be *more* legitimate than a real-world church like Silverlake? Closing up shop is not only a problem in the real world, but it could prove to be a huge problem in the virtual world. Under present circumstances, it's probably easier to quit playing virtual church — close down the website, turn off the streaming media, and sell your Second Life parcel — than it is to close up a church in the real world.[19] This presents a sticky situation for virtual churches, however, since the person who pastors or programs a virtual church often "owns" the church, so to speak.[20] And that person owns not just the virtual building but also the connections between the virtual churchgoers. If a real-world church closes, members of the church could still meet at the old building at their regular time of worship and decide what to do next to remain a church. But in the virtual world, when a virtual church closes, there is no "where" for the people to meet; the defunct church has irrevocably created spiritual orphans. The creation of more and more unconnected churches born of a desire for radical decentralization and collaboration can result only in more and more spiritually orphaned people. One thing we do know: this is antithetical to the Bible's view of the church (Rom. 12:5).

Is there no way to create collaborative virtual churches that have both authority and legitimacy? To some degree, an early hope for this may be the internet campuses of megachurches; virtual church-goers could safely look to the mother church to provide accountability for their internet campus. Still, I fear that in much larger and much wilder parts of the virtual world such as Second Life, many people will gravitate toward virtual-world churches that look pretty but lack legitimacy and authority. Maybe there really are no substantive differences between the real world and the virtual world.

The Jedi Church

Another true story: I know a "pastor" here in San Jose who had a one-hit wonder in the 1980s and now has a "church" that meets in coffee shops. Maybe he's legit, but I do know his website is all about money, money, money. One of his followers tried to attend my church for a while until she found out we wouldn't allow her to channel the spirits of dead people as a ministry to help locate missing children. All things considered, I can't recommend this man's church to people; I question not only aspects of its authority but also its purpose and theology (if it even has a recognizable one). To me, this example goes even deeper into the issues we're talking about than the examples of Silverlake or Second Presbyterian. While it is very easy for people to get sucked into these kinds of "churches" in the real world, isn't it even easier to get bamboozled in the virtual world? Or not?

I fear that if real-world denominations and leaders don't start paying more attention to the virtual world (which means more than putting up a website), this neglect will likely spawn an exponential theological crisis not just for virtual churches but for real-world churches as well. We know that more and more average people are looking for truth outside "organized religion." Christopher Helland demonstrates in his research that when people enter the virtual world with spiritual questions and can't find satisfactory answers from official sources, they will not stop looking but will seek the answers from unofficial sources, of which there are many that serve only to mislead or misinform.[21] This goes back to our earlier discussion on making disciples in the virtual world: Googling for spiritual growth can't be good in anyone's book. So what's the best way to stop bad teaching and root out heterodoxy? No, not an inquisition. It seems to me that the best way is to plant healthy, growing local churches with authority and legitimacy that will reach those who are seeking in the virtual world.

Many of the churches I visited in Second Life had signs that read, "Services available upon request." What services? Are these the virtual world's equivalent of European cathedrals, some of which exist only for tourist dollars, or are they Vegas-style Chapels of Love where people can get married as avatars by a virtual Elvis impersonator?[22] Are these churches all about the Linden dollar (L$)? Or are they more deceptive, teaching ideas contrary to the Bible? Social-science researchers of virtual churches and online spirituality have noted that there is a great deal of fluidity and syncretism among Christian theological beliefs in the virtual world.[23] An example is the popularity of mixing the Force from Star Wars with the Holy Spirit of the Bible. It's not that the average church in the real world doesn't have people in them who believe the Holy Spirit really is like the Force; the problem is that computer-mediated communication provides a greater platform to develop that thinking — or even to create a virtual church whose theology is a little bit gospel and whole lot Jedi. ("Use the Holy Spirit, Luke" — sounds good, but it's not biblical.) Heterodoxy has always been a huge problem for real-world churches, and it looks as though it will be an even greater problem for virtual churches.

If we search the virtual world, it becomes apparent that many traditional Christian groups believe that all the church at large needs to do is create a website that gives the correct answers, and then direct people in real-world churches who have lives in the virtual world to surf over to their official answers. Wrong. Information doesn't save anyone, and information on a website is not contextualized for the surfer (Acts 8:31). A website probably will not show a Jedi the error of his or her ways. Only the living proclamation of the truth is suited to change people's lives. The best — dare I say only? — way to proclaim the contextualized truth of the gospel to our world, real or virtual, is through a local church, where a person can experience the difference between the Force and *his* Force. Isn't this the point of "apostolic" ministry? To send the gospel into a new area so as to plant a local church? To teach people the truth of the gospel?

I fear that those who look to the virtual world for a radical reformation of the church misunderstand the importance of authority and legitimacy in planting healthy churches, because they misunderstand the nature of power and the depravity of our souls and the ease with which we are sucked into fictional ideas. For example, one advocate of this new-world church order writes that the church of the future should be "a new global voice in which ideas and imagination, not structural or positional power, moderate religious dialogue" and that "wisdom ... is the new gatekeeper as spiritual community is reborn in a rapidly growing network of conversations."[24] How naive. I'd love to see ideas and imagination run any kind of church, even a virtual one. Let's see what happens when imagination confronts an elder board! Sorry, but whenever humans are involved, there will always be a struggle for power. Humans cannot create a perfectly equal society (or even an Acts 2 society, as it is frequently misinterpreted to mean) where there is not some degree of authority. Andrew Jones explains the situation well: virtual churches and ministries "saw power flow to the margins, to the 'others' in society who did not have a voice in the previous hierarchies. But once those people find their voice and gain their congregation, the flow of power stays with them rather than flows out in equal measure."[25] We want to make sure the power stays with advocates of a historic, Christian faith, not a Christian Jedi master. I believe we in the church have a responsibility to see as many virtual churches planted with authority and legitimacy — and with God's blessing — as possible.

Mark Brown of Anglican Cathedral in Second Life speaks to his congregation during a worship service.

Every time you buy software, download an update, or join a web group, you're prompted to click the check box that says you agree with the EULA, or End User License Agreement, of the program or group. This agreement — actually a legal contract — basically says that you will use the program the way "they" want you to, and stipulates a lot of things you can't do with "their" program.[26] While EULAs can be burdensome at times, they also help to bridge the authority gap by letting the end user know the parameters of the use of the program. If one of the great needs of virtual churches is to have greater legitimacy, how do they create this greater legitimacy with their end users? And how do they promote collaboration without encouraging people to act as spiritual orphans? Can virtual churches establish healthy parameters?

To have a productive dialog, let's distinguish between two words that people use to describe what they see as the future of virtual churches as it relates to authority: *decentralized* and *participatory*. A decentralized church is one that moves power from a central hierarchy to local groups or individuals. Decentralization can be good as long as it doesn't create spiritual orphans. A participatory church is one that fully includes smaller groups and individuals in the being and doing of church. These words are related, but they do have independent meanings. Since it seems likely that many virtual churches will be more decentralized than the average real-world church, we must ask, Is this a good thing? Is it biblical?

Most of the examples I gave earlier in this chapter caution virtual churches to weigh just how decentralized they should be. For those readers who come from hierarchical Christian denominations and who see the great freedom of the virtual world as a breath of fresh air, decentralization could be a good thing, if used wisely. But when the decentralization of churches becomes extreme or naive, it will more than likely result in unsatisfactory consequences. On the other hand, creating virtual churches that are highly participatory would probably be a very good thing (1 Peter 2:5, 9). Anything virtual churches can do to get people out of the virtual pew and into kingdom-building endeavors is always a good thing. Instead of tearing down hierarchies, it seems far better for virtual churches to focus on becoming incredibly participatory, even leading the way in this regard and spilling this ideal over into real-world churches.

There are several ways that virtual churches can strike a balance between hierarchy and complete decentralization, and yet strive to be fully participatory, and they can do so in such a way that they can probably rival real-world churches.

One way is to create a clear EULA-like agreement between people and the church as an organization in order to build understanding and trust.[27] For example, Second Life has a EULA, but it is so much legalese that it is inaccessible to the average person. As a result, even though Second Life is a place where anyone can do anything, even be their own God,[28] residents treat Lindens (Second Life moderators) as capricious deities; they are met with a lot of suspicion and hostility. (In their own world — imagine that! Think of the theological implications!)[29] The reason is obvious: there is a disconnection — an opacity — between the world of the programmer (priest) and the Second Life citizen (lay person). Instead of just assuming that virtual churchgoers know how to do virtual church and get the code and the secret handshake, virtual churches need to take extra steps not needed in the real world to create extra avenues for participation (which probably also would help with legitimacy).

Among both virtual- and real-world organizations, virtual churches could lead the way in transparency. My younger brother, Jason, a marketing professional in the high-tech industry, emailed me something profound: maybe the greatest implication of computer-mediated communication for virtual churches (and the church at large) is *not* that the church can better mass-communicate its message to people around the world but that the church can become more transparent than ever in its history, allowing people around the world to use the virtual world as a way to taste and see if the church really is from God. Everyone from the Masons to the Mormons to Mensa mass-communicates their schtick but hides their secrets. In the virtual world, the church has the power to trump any other organization not by communicating ideology but by practicing transparency. Bobby Gruenewald echoes this idea when he says that "transparency, and real authenticity — letting people understand who you are and not [casting] some sort of secret corporate veil over everything — is a critical need for the church."[30] Transparency can create a greater sense of legitimacy, collaboration, and openness in how virtual churches communicate to people in the virtual world.

Another way to encourage transparency and authenticity is to create an organization or group that will help brand healthy, legitimate virtual churches and internet campuses. In the 1970s, a number of governmental and Christian leaders felt the need for financial accountability for large national ministries that take donations, so they founded the ECFA (Evangelical Council of Financial Accountability). Now, when anyone in my church asks me if they should give money to such-and-such organization, one of the questions I always ask is whether the ministry is ECFA certified. Even more to the point, when people are looking for a church in San Jose, and they don't want to attend mine for whatever reason, I am pretty aware of which churches would be a good fit and which would not. The reason is that I can see what organization these groups and these churches are with, and I can make a good judgment call. I'm sure we can all agree that anything that promotes understanding with virtual seekers is a good situation for everyone.

It is critical for the virtual world of the immediate future — a world which will be a lot less Wild West than the virtual world of today — that virtual churches be planted with full legitimacy and authority. Virtual churches must develop a demonstrable legitimacy if they are to grow into significant and healthy churches, because future generations won't look at involvement in the virtual world as something that only mavericks do. This is great, because most people don't want to go to church with mavericks. Look at any 1950s Western — there's always the sheriff, the gunslinger, the cattle baron, the posse, but in most scenes there are a lot more timid townsfolk than anyone else. Many people will want to attend virtual churches that are not maverick or avant-garde but are solid, orthodox, and faithful to God's calling. In fact, the group dynamics of virtual churches will require a large degree of normality and consistency if virtual churches are to survive and grow.[31]

WikiWorship Revisited

Last chapter, we started talking about the power of decentralized, or "wiki," worship. Again, *wiki* doesn't mean decentralized, though it implies it. The word entered into our virtual lexicon primarily due to the founding of Wikipedia by Jimmy Wales in 2001. Wikipedia is an open-source virtual encyclopedia that is "quicker" than printed encyclopedias like Britannica because it is continually being added to; it's fundamentally different from Britannica because it's collaborative and decentralized. The result is that Wikipedia dwarfs all print encyclopedias in size; thus it seems to hold great promise.

Wikipedia is an ingenious but dreadful idea. No, it is — let me explain. Wikipedia is like telemarketing, income taxes, and pann-scan full-screen DVDs — things that seemed like a good idea to make life better but that really made it worse. Wikipedia is ingenious because it's a little bit addictive, a little bit useful, a little bit worthwhile, and at the top of every Google search page. It's dreadful because it can be terribly inaccurate and an unreliable source of information. In many ways, Wikipedia is the Russian roulette of information gathering: five out of six tries will yield useful and correct information, but it's the sixth one that will kill you, though you'll never know which one was the killer. In its present form, Wikipedia is akin to the *Weekly World News* tabloid — a very strange mix of fact, fiction, and opinion.[32] Let's hope its standards continue to evolve.

While there are lots of problems with Wikipedia, the biggest is the conflation of information with wisdom. Even though I can find some articles on Wikipedia that are factually accurate, that doesn't mean that those articles did justice to their subject matter. Wikipedia may have more information, but as a whole, Britannica is superior because it takes into account not just information but interpretation, context, and wisdom. Sometimes knowing what not to say is more important than repeating all of the information available on a subject.

In chapter 4, we talked about the power of feedback loops for virtual discipleship. Wikipedia works on a similar principle: user-generated content in an environment that allows for smart construction and updating. This raises an important question: how do we know that we have good information — or better yet, wisdom — in our loop? This is a problem in both the real and virtual worlds. I believe this is where authority and legitimacy must come into play: if virtual churches are fully decentralized, no one is guiding the feedback loops of the people in the church. Some will argue they will be self-guiding, but I don't see much evidence in church history that full decentralization ever worked. Virtual churches must find a balance between user-generated (decentralized) and user-directed (participatory) experiences. Without authority and legitimacy, people will gather to be the participative church without the possibility of mentored formative spiritual growth. I'm not arguing for a priestly hierarchy; I'm arguing for Augustine's ladder of wisdom, where information is second to wisdom and spiritual formation.[33]

At this point, evidence suggests that many traditional Christian denominations are not interested in fully engaging the virtual world.

Whether or not they realize it, new virtual churches need traditional denominations' received wisdom and tradition to create the best, next-wave churches. Anecdotally, I went to the main websites of two different Protestant denominations: one that prides itself on being influential and evangelistic, and one that, based on its handling of basic truths of the faith (such as those found in the Nicene Creed), I consider theologically orthodox only with reservations. The questionable group has a vibrant virtual presence, with at least several active virtual churches. The theologically solid but prideful denomination? None that I could see, not to mention a really bad, information-driven website. In the virtual world, "content is abundant but context is not" (Acts 8:31).[34] Virtual churches need more orthodox denominations and church leaders to stop sitting on the sidelines and allowing the gunslinging mavericks to control the spirituality of the virtual world — before it's too late.

chapter 7

Synthetic Sin

The first thing I noticed about LifeChurch.tv in Second Life is that a number of women wore lingerie to church.

Well, at least their avatars wore lingerie. Now that you've got that image stuck in your head, consider that for all I know, the lingerie-clad avatars were really thirty-eight-year-old single guys lounging around in their pj's in their parents' homes attending virtual church while their moms cooked them chocolate-chip waffles for a late, second breakfast. Does that make it worse, or better? At least he or she or whatever went to church, right?

The first time I attended LifeChurch.tv Internet Campus, I stayed really focused on worship and participation. (And, yes, if you must know, I *was* in my pj's — something I have not yet done in my real-world church, though I do wonder if it would make me more approachable.) After attending the internet campus a few times, I got the hang of LifeChurch.tv's virtual console and was able to multi-task. I decided to hang out in the open forum during worship to see what people were chatting about.

"GOD IS THE DEVIL!!!" screamed Guest_10628. "I HATE GOD!!!"

Guest_10628 wasn't the only one talking, but he or she or whatever sure was the loudest. And the most obnoxious. He continued like this for a while. A few regulars tried to calm the situation, and eventually the "guest" either got bored or was booted. People like Guest_10628 have been a fixture of virtual churches since their inception; I think you must be doing something right when griefers, ragers, and trolls are invading your church's virtual space.[1]

Far more interesting to me was a quieter and far less obtrusive conversation going on between several IC worshipers. It was a conversation about biblical prophecy—a topic that normally invites some shouting.

As I listened in, one virtual worshiper was explaining to several other attendees that according to a prophecy in the Bible, God had ordained either the nation of the Philippines or the Filipino people to destroy Islamic terrorism. This "prophet" requested prayers from other attendees that God would raise up this faithful Filipino fighting force. I'm something of a Bible scholar myself, but this was all news to me.

I couldn't tell by the responses whether the responders believed the prophecy or were just humoring the guy. No one challenged him, which seemed surprising given the ferociousness that virtual theological debates are known for. In almost every way it was just like in a real-world church when a Sunday-morning visitor monologs over coffee and donuts about how God spoke to him about his calling to be the next Enoch, and everyone else just smiles and says, "Oh, okay," hoping desperately that a pastor will come by or a random wormhole will open up for them to escape through (or through which "Enoch" will be taken to heaven).

Speaking of which, it's easy to point to examples of all the unorthodox behavior that goes on in virtual churches—avatars in lingerie, questionable prophets with Christian conspiracy theories, and marauding trolls. Come to think of it, it's easy to do the same with real-world churches too. Church in the virtual world sounds just like church in the real world — lots of confused and broken people who "share" their confusion and brokenness with others.

In case there was ever any doubt, let me say that sin is real, not only in the real world but in the virtual world as well. We know sin exists in Las Vegas, Amsterdam, and Rio de Janeiro because movies, advertising, and the news constantly remind us of this. You could even say these cities built their reputations on it. Every time we look in our spam folders or mistakenly visit an inappropriate website, we are reminded that sin exists in the virtual world in a big way. Some people are even hoping that the virtual world will build its reputation on it — that the virtual world will be the most sinful place on earth.

How will the church respond? Heads in the sand? Throw up some John 3:16 billboards on the virtual highway to hell? Or roll up its sleeves and engage a world ripe for the gospel?

 How can virtual churches confront sin and brokenness in the virtual world? What are the ethical issues facing virtual churches?

In this chapter, I'm going to do something I don't really like to do, but it's a must. I'm going to use the word *sin* more the way culture uses it — being naughty, doing bad things — instead of the way the Bible uses it.[2] I decided to do this because our culture's definition is less nuanced and therefore is a little easier to get a handle on during our brief time together. This way we won't debate whether avatars in lingerie worshiping in church is sin in the biblical sense; we can just agree it's a problem that virtual churches face. At the same time, we can still apply many of the implications of this broad idea of sin to more precise and nuanced instances of sin.

The virtual world reveals that sin is alive, well, and not limited to our physical bodies. Of course, Christians have always known this (Matt. 5:28). No one needs a body to disobey God or act unethically; our hearts and minds are fully capable of sinning even if our bodies never go through with it. In some cases, computer-mediated communication has greatly exacerbated the power of sin in both worlds. Is sin in the virtual world really any different from sin in the real world? Either way, how will the church respond?

Testing the TOS

Let's talk about sin. The virtual world's full of it. We all know about the destructive power of online pornography and internet gambling, and the greed of scammers like the rich diplomat's widow from Nigeria who just needs to borrow your bank account, thereby netting you a six-million-dollar reward for your assistance. As new waves of technological innovation enter the virtual world, the colors and flavors of sin will continue to grow. In some poor parts of the world, virtual sweatshops have opened, paying very low wages for workers to create virtual products such as designer clothing for rich avatars.[3] The world's first virtual millionaire, Anshe Chung, made her money in virtual real estate but got her business going by being a "black mistress" at the Cannabis Cathedral.[4] Most virtual worlds, such as Second Life and The Sims, have their own *Sopranos*-style mafia and organized crime syndicates.[5] One Everquest 2 player cheated the system, causing a virtual market crash, and then laundered over a hundred thousand dollars into the real world in three weeks.[6] Hate-based attacks, such as a recent one against a group of sexual-assault survivors in Second Life (and including those against Christians), are becoming more targeted and more sophisticated.[7] Internet addiction has become more widespread and is now recognized as a dysfunction by many psychologists worldwide; one infamous Korean couple was so addicted to their virtual-world lives that at night they left their infant sleeping alone in their apartment while they played World of Warcraft at the internet cafe, only to come home the next morning to find the infant had suffocated to death.[8]

We could go on and on with other examples, but the problem here is that the virtual world suffers from the same kind of alarmist news reporting that plagues our real world. If the virtual world makes the news, it's not because someone rescued someone else's virtual pet or because someone loved their virtual neighbor; it's almost always because of some tawdry scandal or something even more bizarre and reprobate. The most famous example is Julian Dibbell's "A Rape in Cyberspace," a story that ignited the first virtual news cycle.[9] We can also look at the fact that almost half of the news stories about the groundbreaking Church of Fools virtual church focused primarily on invading trolls and uninvited Satan worshipers.[10] There are even books, such as *The Second Life Herald*, that feature virtual child porn and pimps on the cover, to say nothing of the exaltation of sleaze inside their covers.[11] The result of alarmist news reporting is largely a skewed perspective on the virtual world that neo-Luddites in the church at large are happy to point out. Yes, sin exists in the virtual world just as it does in the real world, but in largely the same degree and quantity, even if in different colors and flavors. Every human era (and world) faces the same struggle of sin, law, and grace, just in new situations or new venues.[12]

Popular culture vaunts the virtual world for its freedoms, but in some ways, the virtual world is a lot less free than we think. Anytime we visit a virtual world, open up an email account, or post a book review on Amazon.com, there is always a Terms of Service document, or TOS, lurking in the background. While a EULA is typically a broad, legal document that establishes rights, a TOS frequently targets what a person can and can't do.[13] When a Second Life moderator boots a griefer from Second Life, or Google cancels an email account, it's because of a TOS violation. Just about every product or platform in the virtual world is covered by some type of EULA, TOS, or other legal document, which when you think about it is far more restrictive than anything we face in the real world. In the virtual world, if I grief, I violate the TOS and am booted. In the real world, I can go to Wal-Mart, buy a megaphone, and make a lot of grief and ruckus in my back yard, but it can't get me booted from the real world (unless, perhaps, my neighbor takes justice into his own hands).[14]

At the same time, the nature of the virtual world does recast the issue of sin and freedom. Because the virtual world is a real world where a person is telepresent, it allows and encourages certain types of human agency or action, and discourages other types. Since the virtual world is new, people are still wrestling with the issue of agency and ethical response similar to what happens with the advent of any new technology, just on a much greater scale. Even though the real world doesn't have a TOS or EULA per se, most people — whether or not they realize it or want to admit it — still live their lives by one of several codes that govern their agency and ethics. Some are universal codes (don't jump off cliffs), some are legal (don't steal), some are societal (say please and thank you), some are self-chosen (whoever dies with the most toys wins). The virtual world erases some of these codes, such as "don't jump off cliffs," allowing virtual people to find greater "freedom" — although really the term is *free agency*.[15] The problem really comes in when the virtual world erases certain societal (no more please and thank you) or legal (stealing virtual stuff is okay because it's not real) codes.

The increase in undirected free agency is what will lead to the expected increases in the colors and flavors of sinfulness in the virtual world.[16] As Pope John Paul II predicted, the increasing desire for and exaltation of free agency injures our world at large and empowers sin.[17] In the virtual world, people feel free to speak and act more the way they feel than they do in the real world; virtual-world researchers often call this being "disinhibited."[18] While conventional wisdom holds that the reason people act out more in the virtual world than in the real world is because of their anonymity in the virtual world,[19] it may instead be because they're crying for attention.[20] When parents give children too much free agency to do as they please, these free-range children often act out not because they want to be bad but because they intuitively crave boundaries. Even though it may be that many people flock to the virtual world to be free from the constraints of this world, their avatars will still be limited by some code or teleology — resulting in a real hodgepodge of real-world and virtual-world ethics.

Here's the rub: when free agency is increased, people have a harder time not only figuring out what the codes are but also knowing how much is too much. A big part of the problem is *play*. A number of young adults in my real-world church occasionally invite me to their homes for cookouts or small group times, and each has a Wii at their house. I always ask to play, and they are always surprised that their unhip pastor will do whatever it takes not only to play but to win. It's not that I'm that competitive — okay, maybe I am a little — but it's really easy to get wrapped up in the act of play. Virtual sociologists have found that the more "sinful" an avatar a person picks, the more likely they are to act in a "sinful" manner, so as to *play* the part.[21] If a person creates a shady character online, they are more likely to do shady things, even though these things can have very real consequences. If this is true, what are the implications for the church?

This brings us to the central issue: there is a real uncertainty about ethics online, not just among virtual-world architects and legal scholars but among everyday people.[22] What is worse, a recent survey of virtual-world citizens found that 50 percent of people surveyed don't even believe the virtual world has sin in it.[23] Why? Because it's not *real*.

Here the church is poised to fail big-time — to drop a ball of monumental proportions. Here's how it will play out. As tens of millions of people flock to virtual worlds, traditional Christians who fear change in the church at large will see alarmist headlines about the virtual world and will dismiss the virtual world as one big sinful fantasy, as being not real.[24] They will turn the virtual world over to its own devices, and tens of millions of people — with no true ethical compass — will embrace greater free agency and then write their own rules on what is right and what is wrong.[25] Before long, sin in the virtual world will start to redefine sin in the real world; what's permissible in the virtual world will start to seem less wrong in the real world.[26] After a generation passes, new church leaders will ask, "How did we get into this mess?" This has already started to happen, and there is evidence to suggest it's very close to being too late for the church at large to change.

The solution that many church leaders may propose is either to warn their followers away from the virtual world or to speak *ex cathedra* from their real-world churches. As history demonstrates, neither of these will work. Worse yet, some will turn to boycotts or propose laws.[27] These won't work either. The solution is quite simple. If we want to reach a world for Christ, to turn it away from sin and selfishness back to real freedom and the true peace found only in God, we'll make it happen only by planting churches in that world, to reach and sanctify its people (1 Peter 2:9). For those who doubt, let me prove it: when God wanted to reach the real world, he didn't warn a few followers or speak from his throne; he sent his Son (and Spirit) to be with sinful people (Rom. 5:6). It's only by being with people that we can change people. The only true solution to virtual sin is to send churches into the virtual world.[28]

CyberSanctification

What the virtual world desperately needs is the sanctifying power of the church: its Spirit and its people.[29] Who better to live as ethical and virtuous avatars than the people of God? Unfortunately, it will not be sufficient for Christians to journey individually into the virtual world to affect it; it will require a church to effect real change (1 Peter 2:9). Many, many people venture into virtual worlds because they can rebuild their lives the way they want, something they feel they are powerless to do in the real world. The church offers the one true way to rebuild — to redeem — these folks' lives in both worlds. The best way for the church to confront sin in the virtual world is the same way as in the real world — to demonstrate sin's fruitlessness compared with the gospel.

Let's consider the effect lifelogging has begun to have on the ethics of interpersonal relationships in the most recent wave of virtual-world development. While the church should encourage believers to lifelog their lives as a powerful testimony of kingdom transformation, the simple fact is that many people are lifelogging a ton of sin too. Many young people are going to post photos of their wild college trip to Cancun, only to find out ten years later that a coworker has Googled or Waybacked the photos to use to their advantage. Can or should a church hire an internet campus pastor who, years before becoming a believer, posted salacious photos of their wild partying that now anyone in the church can find if they are so inclined? Before the internet, our tendency (hopefully) was toward grace and forgiveness, but doesn't the constant availability of these incriminating photos change things? Or not? Even though the trip was a long time ago, the photos are still easily accessible today. This is only the tip of the iceberg; as post-digital-revolution generations grow up, comfortable in the virtual world, their virtual-world experience will record both their achievements and peccadilloes.[30] "Information that was once scattered, forgettable, and localized," explains Daniel Solove, "is becoming permanent and searchable."[31]

Do virtual churches have the potential to lead the way in this crisis? Can a virtual church have a far more meaningful and far more potent impact than an average real-world church? It seems likely, through the power of avatar-mediated worship. At my real-world church, we have a registered sex offender who attends irregularly. He's a rough fellow who, by his looks, you'd never want to meet alone at night. As any pastor knows, it's not the easiest situation; he did his time and I wish him the best to pursue God fully in his life, but he knows the deal and chooses to sit by himself and not talk to many people when he is on campus. He's welcome, but his bad decisions affect where he can serve and how people respond to him. His mistakes are legally lifelogged by the state of California for anyone and everyone to see. If he attended a virtual church, there would still be issues, but avatar-mediated worship would allow him freedom to interact and to be a part of the church to a degree not possible in the real world.[32] In the virtual world, he could even write out his testimony on his profile, letting people know of God's amazing grace in his life before they even meet him.[33] Other virtual churchgoers could get to know his heart without judging him by his rough, ex-con exterior.

Even though this is just one small example, virtual churches can exemplify grace and forgiveness for people by bringing down physical walls, increasing the depth of communication, allowing for more ministry freedom, and even granting a new life—or at least a new avatar—to someone whom God has restored. Rather than react to the evolving ethics of the virtual world, can virtual churches set the standard not only for believers but for nonbelievers as well?

Christian Cosplay

Since the dawn of time, many people have wanted to be someone else, and the virtual world has now made it easy to do. The virtual world allows a whole new type of *cosplay*, a euphemism that sort of means "costume play" but is quite a bit more nuanced than that. *Cosplay* comes out of Japanese fantasy culture and involves creating a persona to play out while in costume; the costume defines the role the person plays. With the advent of worlds like Second Life, cosplay takes on a whole new meaning, since the limit is now only the imagination (or programming skills).

When I ask virtual-church pastors, bloggers, and theologians what they consider to be the greatest ethical issue facing virtual churches, the almost unanimous answer is identity. Identity is the focal issue because so many of our other concerns with the virtual world — such as trust and privacy — relate to it. Right now, because it facilitates a lot of undirected free agency, the virtual world is in something of a Wild West phase, in which people are creating the rules, especially those involving identity, as they go along.[34] This won't always be the case; as more and more people access the virtual world, some worlds may purposefully retain anonymity, but most will require more and more identity validation (even if it is kept "private" by the world's ownership team). For the time being, though, it is difficult to know whether the people we meet in virtual worlds are accurately representing themselves, or if their avatars are a mask, in the real-world sense of the word. Let's dig deeper into this issue than we did in chapter 4.

Conventional wisdom holds that people in virtual worlds hide behind the masks of their avatars, using the anonymity granted by their avatars to do things they normally wouldn't do in the real world. This is often the reason people oppose virtual churches; they argue it's impossible to be the people of God if you don't even know who the people are. Douglas Groothuis exemplifies this position: "A masquerade would be easier to execute in the recesses of cyberspace than in face-to-face conversation."[35] But is this true? Any pastor worth their salt knows that when it comes to the church, this argument doesn't hold much water.[36] A candid real-world pastor knows that many, if not most, of the people who come to their church on Sunday hide behind the much more compelling and persuasive real-world masks of comfort, success, or happiness. Don't we sit in churches every Sunday and let our highly developed middle-class masks hide all sorts of sin and brokenness? Compared with the "I'm fine, how about you" church mask, aren't the masks of the virtual world rather obvious, if not transparent?[37]

Masks and identity issues have been around since the world began; they are nothing new to either world.[38] We all use masks from time to time, no matter the world in which we live. The question is, Are masks wrong or bad or unbiblical? Are they acceptable in some situations? If I choose to hide part of my identity in the real world, is it bad or sinful? How about if I choose to hide part of my identity in the virtual world? I suspect that more of us would think that a problem. Why? Let's take it a step farther. What if I choose an avatar in Second Life that is a younger, more handsome version of myself? Am I hiding? Is it bad? Is it sinful?[39] What if I choose an avatar that is a robot? Is that bad? Is it sinful? Most people would probably think that either of these two avatars is probably harmless. But what if I choose a female robot for an avatar? Is that bad or sinful? What if I choose a female human avatar that looks like Marilyn Monroe? I suspect a lot of Christians would say, "Yes, these last two are bad," but really, what's the difference? All four of these avatars are inaccurate representations of me; they're all masks. Why is representing myself as a more handsome me or a robot somehow more acceptable or more right than representing myself as a female robot or a woman?[40] Even more important, should a virtual church accept me if I have a handsome or robotic avatar, but turn me away if I have a female avatar?

Identity is a big issue for several reasons. According to the modern Western worldview, masks are false not because they are inherently wrong or bad but because they are not based on empirical, external evidence. In other words, masks are bad not because they hide people but because they may provide inaccurate information and may offer inaccurate representations of people. So does this mean that the more accurately I represent myself, the better everything is? I'm not at all convinced this is a biblical perspective. For whatever reason, the Bible doesn't really discuss masks or representational choices; it discusses only outright deception (Prov. 24:28). It is no more accurate to represent myself as a robot than as a woman — both are fully inaccurate. Is either one more deceptive than the other? Again, we must be careful here; it is cultural, not biblical, to suggest that a man who represents himself as a robot is somehow being less deceptive than a man who represents himself as a woman. The only difference seems to be that if I represent myself as a robot, everyone knows I'm not really a robot, whereas if I represent myself as a woman, not everyone knows it.

Is it really deceptive and wrong for a man to have a female avatar? This is a really hard question to ask without trying to assign a motive. Is it less wrong for a person in a real-world church to wear a middle-class mask than it is for a person in a virtual-world church to wear a gender mask? The middle-class mask is not necessarily less damaging to the person, and the gender mask is not necessarily less transparent. If we want to be strictly biblical, I think we can say only that a mask in and of itself is outside of God's will when its sole purpose is to deceive, though I would tend to think that all masks are not a part of God's perfect plan for anyone.[41] Therefore, it is hard to prove that my choosing a female avatar is necessarily any worse than my "dressing up" in an uncomfortable suit and tie and going to listen to a concert of classical music with a smile on my face. (Talk about a mask!) While there will always be people in the virtual world who intend to deceive (just as in the real world), most people don't choose avatars with that purpose in mind.[42] This includes, in many cases, even the highly contentious issue of men with female avatars (and vice versa). Unfortunately, neither physical presence nor telepresence seem to be antidotes to the problems raised by identity. What can the church do?

CROSS-GENDERED AVATARS

The issue of men using female avatars — and its rightness or wrongness — is currently the subject of intense debate inside and outside the church. Many Christians I have spoken with who object to the virtual world as a whole always seem to bring this issue up. They feel that a man who represents himself as a woman is at best dishonest and at worst a pervert.

A big problem is perception. A man can choose an asexual avatar such as a robot or an alien, and no one will question it, but when a man chooses a female avatar, it raises eyebrows (especially in the church).

Still, there is evidence that when a man chooses a female avatar, it is for one of several reasons that deal with sexual issues. Studies and anecdotes indicate one reason men may select female avatars is for the purpose of sexual role play and experimentation. Another reason is to work out internal gender issues. A final reason I have found in my experience is that some men who go for female avatars often are lonely or are severely deficient in their real-world interaction and relationships with women, or are even scared of women, and they replace real-world relationships with real-world women with their female avatars. Remember, most people see an avatar not only as an extension of themselves but also as someone slightly distinct — maybe like a child's imaginary friend.

This issue is not limited to the virtual world; we see these same issues play out in the real world. I have firsthand testimony from people in the virtual world for whom the virtual world hurt, although in many cases helped, them with their relationship and gender issues. In order to reach people with cross-gendered avatars in the virtual world, virtual churches must not jump to conclusions but should treat each person as a person whom Christ died for.

Finally, women do use male avatars, but their rationale appears to be different — to avoid getting hit on by men, especially in gaming virtual worlds — or at least their doing so is more acceptable to the church and the culture.

The people of God have to decide whether the time they spend in the virtual world is missional or one big cosplay. What masks do we put on when we venture into the virtual world? If any deceptive representation of ourselves is outside of God's plan for our lives, should virtual churches discourage not only cross-gender avatars but also robotic or even overly beautiful avatars? Should we select avatars that will honor God, or avatars that make us feel most comfortable? Should virtual churches permit people to worship with avatars dressed in lingerie, with offensive forum names, or with cross-gendered avatars? Are virtual churches launching in the virtual world because it's fun to wear masks and play church? More important, are real-world churches merely creating religious cosplay by launching internet campuses in order to gain followers or money? The simplest and surest way to determine whether a church is playing games or building the kingdom is to consider how that church, virtual or real, handles its identity (whether it's transparent and accessible, or secretive and insular), and from that what steps, if any, it takes to build trust and protect privacy among its members and guests. For the church to be the church in the virtual world, it has to have the most transparent identity in the virtual world.

This brings us back to what we talked about in the previous chapter. Churches expect people to divulge information about themselves, though at the same time many senior pastors will not even post their email address on their church's webpage. To establish themselves (for the Anglican Cathedral, for example, to distinguish itself from the Cannabis Cathedral in Second Life), virtual churches must be willing to make their identities fully known to people in the virtual world. It seems to make sense that legitimacy for virtual churches will come through honesty, authenticity, and transparency. In fact, virtual churches probably will have to be more transparent than real-world churches to gain the trust of people in both worlds. Virtual churches can do this if their identities, and the identities of their people, are on full display. In the virtual world, one click of the mouse can reveal everything a virtual church or internet campus chooses to make known to the rest of the world. Transparency can change the way the church is the church in the virtual world — and in the real world.

The task ahead for virtual churches is to sanctify the virtual world through their commitment to integrity and holiness. As we discussed in the previous chapter, there are little things that virtual churches can do to improve the safety and security of virtual-church worship. Stefano Pace provides a great example of that in a recent article. Pace explains that virtual churches, like virtual businesses, can use seals of approval, branding, supraleveraged technology, and reputation systems as a first step to engender trust and to encourage godliness in virtual-world worship.[43] In the end, the virtual world is a fallen world just like the real world. Naive alarmists will try to convince us that the virtual world is somehow worse or more sinful than the real world,[44] but this is one of the Enemy's oldest tricks to prevent the spread of the kingdom of God. Virtual churches are just like any other church in any other world. As sin abounds, let it be Christ's church reaching out to its world.

The Internet Campus

Just because you've thrown together a few buildings doesn't mean you have a campus.

My first salaried job after college was working as a chemist at a large biotech company with a corporate presence in Research Triangle Park, North Carolina. They had hired me for work times that didn't interfere with my seminary class schedule, and since the job involved using advanced instrumentation with funny names to test for minute quantities of illegal drugs, it seemed sure to beat working in the seminary cafeteria serving sloppy joes for six bucks an hour. Because it was my first "real" job, it was exciting to be shown around the company's "campus" and be introduced to many of the different labs and projects housed in the corporate complex.

Within a really short amount of time, any excitement I felt about working there dimmed and winked out of existence. Even though the company landscaped its grounds and positioned its buildings to look like a campus, there really was no interaction between the buildings, or any fun, central meeting places for employees. It was just several, individual office buildings grouped together. I found out pretty quickly that my security access card opened only the door to my lab, the workers' snack room, and the side entrance to my building; it wouldn't even open the front door because the front door wasn't for employees.[1] To make matters worse, I worked at night, so there were fewer workers on campus than at other times. Even though my lab supervisor preferred I not leave campus on breaks, I regularly sneaked out with one of my lab mates to hang out at a twenty-four-hour sandwich shop. The work environment was just too sterile and depressing.

Not every campus environment is as flawed as the one I experienced — for example, the Apple campus in Silicon Valley. Last time I visited the Apple campus, I met my friend Chris, an engineer on the Mac team, for lunch there. As I turned left into 1 Infinite Loop, drove toward the big Apple, and parked beside a car with a "WWSJD" license plate, I noticed that Apple looks like a typical grouping of nice tech buildings in any industrial park. But inside I found that it's quite a bit more. Once I cleared security, Chris and I exited out the back of Building 1 and entered the campus quad. Though we just went to the gourmet cafe to have lunch, we could have chatted at the coffee bar, played basketball on the pro court, or just sat at the picnic tables on the manicured lawn with other Apple employees and guests. Apple uses the quad for more than just playing hacky sack during the day; some afternoons they have concerts by big-name rock stars on the quad for their employees.

Now, I'm not one of those rabid Apple fans — the ones you see perpetually sitting in Starbucks with all the protruding white wires. Mostly it's because I prefer that my hardware run more like the Millennium Falcon than some gleaming white alien art form. And while I don't want to make it sound like working at Apple is all sunshine and lollipops (it's not), Apple does have a really nice campus — a far cry from the "campus" of the biotech company I worked for in seminary. The Apple campus connects people and creates meaningful campus life. A real campus can make a big difference when it comes to building real community.

As we have discussed, there is a rapidly growing interest in virtual churches, or perhaps more specifically in leveraging the power of the internet to get more people to connect to a church in the virtual world. Think about the evolution of websites in the past couple of decades. In the early 1990s, some churches explored the idea of having a website alongside of their regular ministry. By the mid- to late-nineties, every church *had* to have a website to be doing anything cool in ministry. I'll admit it: when I was looking for a pastoral job in 2000 after running out of money trying to finish my PhD studies, I didn't apply for a church ministry position at any church that didn't have a website. My logic at the time was that any church without a website in 2000 was too far out of date. Now millions of church websites hastily thrown up in the '90s litter the virtual world. They looked bad then, and they look positively prehistoric by today's standards. It seems that many of these websites didn't live up to their hype, just as the biotech campus I worked on didn't live up to the hype it got during my interview process. How can churches today design internet campuses in the virtual world that are more than just a bunch of virtual buildings linked together?

 What must a church do to turn a jumble of digital content into an internet campus? What are the ingredients of healthy virtual-campus life?

As churches turn to the virtual world to plant churches and minister, they need to do more than create virtual ministry spaces, upload spiritual content, and decide how to perform virtual baptism. They need a commitment as deep and sincere as the commitment to start a church in the real world. And they need to take a hard look at what creates healthy campus life in the virtual world.

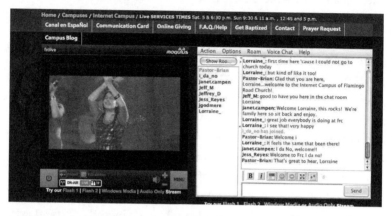

Live worship and discussion at Flamingo Road Church's internet campus.

iPastors

The hottest pastoral commodity in the next few years may not be the worship pastor or the small groups pastor but the virtual-church pastor — the iPastor. Many churches will see this as the "next big thing" and hire accordingly. To survive and thrive, virtual churches need pastors who can shepherd a telepresent flock in the virtual world. Since seminaries don't exactly offer degrees in virtual-church ministry, and there are not many experienced virtual-church pastors on the job market, what will all of these churches do? Even more important, how will these churches define *iPastor*?

It will be tempting for well-meaning traditional churches to see the virtual-church pastor as simply the next generation of webmaster; they will look inside their congregations for someone who knows how to set up a static IP address or hack an iPhone. But a webmaster is to a virtual-church pastor as a museum curator is to an artist. A webmaster is the person who organizes and posts digital content, but a virtual-church pastor is the person who not only creates the content but also guides campus life and shepherds the church, a spiritual gathering of real people. A webmaster affects people indirectly, but an iPastor engages people directly. Many newly minted virtual-church pastors of the early twenty-first century will not be solo or lead pastors; many will be associate pastors on staff at larger churches. They will relate to other staff the way a campus pastor or a student ministries pastor or a singles pastor might relate. As such, I think we can all agree that an iPastor should fit the general, biblical qualifications for a pastor.[2] What about technological know-how? Should churches hire virtual-church pastors for their technical skills or for their ministry skills?

Since a virtual church is a real church, not a play church, it must have a real pastor, not a play pastor. A church leadership team doesn't hire a student ministries pastor based solely or primarily on their rapport with youth; they hire the person based primarily on their calling and ministry gifts and only secondarily on their being tragically hip enough to relate to teenagers. In the same way, a church should hire a virtual-church pastor for their calling and gifts and only secondarily for their tech skills. In their enthusiasm to plant virtual churches and internet campuses, churches must not make the mistake of hiring virtual-church pastors who are tech savvy but ministry obtuse. Brian Vasil, one of the very first iPastors using the internet-campus model, warns that most churches he talks with about virtual-church ministry seem intent on hiring a "tech whiz." "It's okay if [virtual-church pastors have] a technological mind," says Vasil, but it's more important that virtual-church pastors "have a heart for people. It has to be good enough for that pastor to love on people that he may never hug or shake hands with ... they have to have a heart for people first."[3] As we have seen all along, virtual churches are not that different from real-world churches. To be successful, virtual-world pastors need the same characteristics as real-world pastors. If churches want to truly engage people in the virtual world, they cannot underestimate the shepherding and ministry requirements of virtual churches. The biggest challenge facing virtual-church pastors is not dealing with technology; it's dealing with people.[4]

Binary Relationships

Like traditional pastoral ministry, virtual-church pastoral ministry will hinge on how the pastor handles people, relationships, and community far more than on how he manages technology. To be successful, a virtual-church pastor has to be more than the church's virtual custodial engineer. My first paid youth pastorate was at a little country church in a particularly eccentric part of rural North Carolina. I took this church instead of others because it had been looking for a youth pastor for a very long time. When I arrived, no one (including me) really knew what I was supposed to do outside of some traditional things like start a youth group. The senior pastor, who was on his fifth or sixth church after retirement, never knew how to describe me exactly; he would tell people from the pulpit to go see "that youth man" if they needed anything. If a church with both real-world and virtual-world campuses views its internet-campus pastor as simply "that tech person" — the job description includes reloading printer drivers or restoring the staff's email — and people are unsure exactly what "that tech person" does, the church will likely miss the mark for planting a healthy virtual church.

Part of the challenge for real-world churches that wish to launch virtual churches is to perceive the internet campus in light of the church's vision and overall plan rather than as a ministry feature such as radio broadcasting or podcasting. It's one thing for a senior pastor to green-light a fourteen-year-old to create a church YouTube video, but it's a whole 'nother thing to green-light the same kid to create and lead an internet campus. In chapter 6, we asked whether a church is really a church if it doesn't have a real pastor. We can take this question a step farther: what kind of virtual church exists when led by a "pastor" who is unskilled in ministry? Churches must find a way to raise skilled virtual-church pastors who have the blessing (and authority) of the church (or denomination or organization) standing behind them.

Second, and more important, to be successful, a virtual-church pastor must have the skills to coach, guide, teach, and encourage people who connect to the church through virtual-world relationships. It's hard enough to lead people in the real world; leading volunteers in the virtual world seems more daunting in just about every way. Think of it like this: email is a quick mode of communication, but it can also be an ineffective and even treacherous one. It's largely ineffective when we try to communicate emotions; it's downright treacherous when we try to communicate suggestions, challenges, or anything disputable. Email makes it easy for misunderstandings to creep in, and misunderstandings are a great stumbling block to pastoral ministry.[5] It would seem that misunderstanding might be the norm in virtual churches. Somehow, virtual-church pastors have to find a way to establish not just real but meaningful relationships with people whom they may never meet in person.

This is a double-edged sword — virtual-church pastors must find a way to minister to people who choose to engage in "optional relationships" in their virtual worlds. These relationships are low-commitment to the point that they often take on binary features. A binary system is 1/0, I/O, on/off. Because of the nature of the virtual world, many of the initial relationships in virtual churches will struggle to go beyond binary: two people will share their deepest, darkest secrets for a time (1, I, on), and then after a few days one or both of the friends will get bored and never log on again (0, O, off). How can virtual-church pastors discourage optional relationships and help people develop solid, healthy community? What kind of virtual-church environment will encourage virtual churchgoers to go "full on" in their virtual-church communities? Can virtual-church pastors generate a healthy campus life designed to build community and not create merely linked ministry spaces? If so, it's their heart for people and shepherding skills, not their technical skills, that will make it happen. It requires a real pastor to turn optional relationships into real community, to build not just ministry spaces but real community in meaningful campus life.

Resource Resolution

Real-world churches that decide to plant virtual churches, especially those using the internet-campus model, will need to size up a number of staffing, organizational, and financial issues and plan how to handle them. While some churches or organizations may be hesitant to hire a full-time virtual-church pastor, there is a sizeable risk in hiring someone to be, say, "student ministries/internet campus pastor" (besides the problems associated with slash pastors in general). Based on my research, I fear that many churches that do so will underestimate the unique pastoral demands on virtual-church pastors. For example, Brian Vasil explains, "I get prayer requests twenty-four hours a day in languages I don't even speak.... I think that's the most valuable thing an internet campus can do is just be there 24/7 for people who need it, worldwide." This 24/7 approach to ministry sounds awesome on paper, but how can churches implement it in a healthy way? Should churches hire a pastor who does nothing but sit in front of the computer twenty-four hours a day, seven days a week chatting with people?[6] This is a big question for virtual churches that closely follow a social connectivity model for virtual church, such as i-church.[7] Will real-world churches pay staff pastors less because their job is to sit around "just chatting"?

Ah, finally, money — where the rubber meets the road for many churches or church boards. The question on the mind of every church treasurer or CFO is whether the church is really going to pay a full salary to someone who talks on the internet to people or who runs around as an avatar (read: who plays video games). And even more important, if the church staffs its own virtual campus, will serious-minded people come? Serious-minded enough to give money to support the ministry?

Anyone who has done pastoral ministry knows you get what you pay for. Staffing a virtual ministry isn't any different. If you hire a fourteen-year-old techie as your internet-campus pastor, I think you know what you'll get. There's some good news, and there's some bad news. The good news is that it is a whole lot cheaper to build a state-of-the-art worship auditorium in the virtual world than it is in the real world. The bad news is that, at least anecdotally, there seems to be a much lower giving rate among virtual-world churchgoers than real-world churchgoers. There are probably several reasons for this. First, some virtual worlds such as Second Life have their own currency, but the currency is highly devalued compared with most Western currency (dollars or euros, for example). A donation of two hundred and fifty Linden dollars may feel like a sizeable contribution, but given currency exchange rates, the church actually receives less than one US dollar, not even enough to pay the electric bill for recharging the iPastor's iPod for the day. Second, a percentage of virtual churchgoers also attend real-world churches, and this may restrict their giving. Third, a number of well-meaning churches and church leaders still tell society that virtual churches are not real churches, and the people who hear this have less reason to give real money to virtual churches. While some churches have had success with "online giving," most virtual churches have struggled with the trade-off of having lower costs but receiving less money. Many of the virtual-church pastors

I spoke to felt their ministries had to be scaled back a great deal because of a lack of resources.

Will virtual churches eventually drive down the costs of doing church in general in the future? I doubt it. Some people think the virtual world will make everything "cheaper, faster," but we can learn a lesson from the Industrial Revolution. As factories came into existence and manufacturing processes became increasingly automated, more products were produced for sale, but this increase in products simply heightened people's expectations for these products (and created a greater largesse in society). The more "automated" churches become, the more content they will be able to produce, but the more all of this will serve to heighten people's expectations of church "products" and "services." I suspect it will be a wash.

Domain Discipline

Virtual-church pastors who want to create healthy church communities need to find a way to ensure that the campus environment remains healthy as well. In the previous chapter, we talked about some ways in which sin can find a foothold in the virtual world, how "optional relationships" can lead to unhealthy relationships, and the impact of sinfulness in general on virtual churches. We now know the difficult task ahead for leaders of virtual churches in their struggle to build healthy communities. One of the most important resources any church has to promote a healthy campus life is the practice of church discipline. Can a virtual church or internet campus practice church discipline?

The simple answer is yes — nothing prevents an internet campus or a virtual church from practicing church discipline. Many already do practice it in some form. From the Reformation onward, several segments of the Christian church have placed a heavy emphasis on church discipline, including making it one of the marks of the church (in the same ballpark of importance as Communion). But even if it is not considered a mark, it's still an important biblical tool for virtual churches.

Let's begin with what we know about church discipline. Jonathan Wilson defines church discipline "as the identification of sin in the lives of disciples and the actions taken by the disciple community in response."[8] Jesus stated the importance of church discipline for the church (Matt. 18:15 – 20; cf. Matt. 16:18 – 19).[9] In the Bible, there appear to be several reasons for practicing church discipline: protecting biblical truths (Titus 1:13), keeping order among the people (1 Tim. 5:20), and resolving disputes and removing offensive churchgoers (1 Cor. 5:3 – 5; 1 Tim. 1:20). One of the hallmarks of spiritual maturity is undoubtedly the willingness of a person to submit to church discipline (Heb. 13:17). Perhaps the most important truth of church discipline is that its goal is not to punish but to strengthen and restore (2 Tim. 4:2; Titus 1:13).

Even though church discipline was a common practice during the last couple of millennia, it fell out of favor in the twentieth century, for several reasons. One is that many people bought into the modern philosophical ideal of personhood: I as a person have complete freedom, autonomy, and soul competency to do anything I please. When churches try to discipline, modern people typically perceive that the church is trying to limit their freedom and rights rather than trying to coach them to be better disciples.[10] Another reason church discipline fell out of favor is that with the collapse of cultural Christianity in the Western world, many traditional churches and denominations rapidly shrank, and selfishness crept into the church. For example, in the real-world church I pastor, our church's leadership team and I have had to administer discipline in a few instances. Invariably, the people we try to coach to make better decisions choose instead to just leave our church. And invariably, many of these people soon start going to another church as if the attempted discipline were unimportant or just our church's opinion. When I call the senior pastor of the individual's new church to let the pastor know the person has fled from church discipline, the pastor never expresses any solidarity and instead typically sees the situation as our church's problem and not something to get worked up over.

Perhaps the better question to ask is whether virtual churches are able to practice church discipline with any effectiveness. If people run away from church discipline in the real world, what chance does a virtual-world church have at keeping order and tweaking people who take part in unhealthy behavior or even just engage in optional relationships? This presents the possibility of more problems than even real-world churches face. Even though church discipline is not punitive, there should be some bite to it (1 Tim. 5:20). But how can it have bite when people worship together as avatars in the virtual world? (Assuming virtual churches don't require avatars to wear digital scarlet letters.)[11]

Can virtual churches break the stranglehold that success and modern culture seem to have on real-world church discipline by redefining church discipline for the virtual world and creating healthy campus life? What if virtual churches established the biblical ground rules early and used this new form of church to build a metaphor for discipline that works in the virtual world? For this to happen, I believe virtual churches will need to work together rather than against each other (as many real-world churches seem to do). Sharing information is important. For example, let's consider modesty. Most real-world churches don't regularly have to contend with women coming to church in lingerie. Virtual churches do. Should virtual churches speak to this behavior? If so, should they discipline virtual churchgoers who dress their avatars inappropriately? If they discipline such churchgoers, what will prevent those churchgoers from picking another scantily clad avatar and next week attending a different virtual church? It seems to me this can be prevented only by a greater degree of cooperation between virtual churches. Identity also is important;

even if virtual-world providers allow people to remain anonymous, virtual churches need to develop a plan by which virtual churchgoers can take part in *every* faith practice of the church. If virtual-world providers begin mandating better forms of identity verification, as many futurists believe they will, church discipline will become easier for virtual churches to lovingly administer. Virtual pastors and virtual churches can have meaningful ministries if they are willing to establish deep commitments to the virtual-ministry field, to work together to coach people into great lives and great choices for the kingdom of God.

chapter 9

Viral Ministry

The Methodists are coming! The Methodists are coming!

At least that's the way many of the North American frontier people felt in the nineteenth century. They were busy creating a new world in a new place and were surprised (and annoyed) at how quickly some of the people of God leveraged new advances in transportation and communication to bring the good news to them. John Wesley originated the idea of reaching a vast number of people in a new world with a new way of doing ministry, a way that many church leaders of the day frowned upon. Were these new Methodist charges real churches? What impact would they have in a brave new world? What Wesley didn't know is that one day computers would prove that his ministry method was superior to the traditional way.

David Sarnoff, an entrepreneurial pioneer of both radio and television and an executive at RCA and NBC, developed an axiom in the 1930s that explained the communicative value of broadcast networks. Sarnoff's Law, as it came to be known, is that "the value of a network is proportional to the number of its members." The more members a network has, the greater the value of the network. On a chart, it's a straight line that gradually slopes upward. This is the standard for broadcast media today — the more listeners or viewers a program has, the more value it has, and the more advertising revenue it can bring in — and perhaps, inadvertently, it is an axiom of megachurch growth — the more attendees a church has, the more money it will have for specialized ministries.

In the early 1970s, Robert Metcalfe, the inventor of Ethernet technology — the most common type of cable-connection standard currently in use to connect computers and network devices — realized that the value of communication networks would soon grow much faster than Sarnoff predicted. In light of the fact that anyone with a telephone or a computer could dial up anyone else with a telephone or computer, he argued that "the value of a network grows in proportion to the square of the number of users." While one telephone is useless, ten telephones have a value of a hundred, and ten thousand telephones have a value of one hundred million.[1] Metcalfe's Law, as it also came to be known, was a driving force behind the internet boom of the late twentieth century. Businesses based their growth on his law and didn't worry about profits; they cared only about creating value. The problem, though, was that a lot of people still cared about profits.

Even as Metcalfe's Law fell out of favor in the early twenty-first century, David Reed, a creator of internet protocols and a software pioneer, argued that Metcalfe was wrong because he underestimated the power of social networking in the virtual world. Reed's Law states that "the utility of large networks, particularly social networks, can scale exponentially with the size of the network."[2] While Sarnoff's Law predicts a straight line of gradual growth, and Metcalfe's Law predicts a line that sharply slopes upward, Reed's Law predicts a line of exponential growth rocketing upward. While several recent theorists have tried to throw doubt on Metcalfe's and Reed's ideas, especially in light of the dot-com bust, Reed developed his law in 1999, before the bust but also before the advent of MySpace and Facebook, recent second-wave virtual-world social networking applications growing at exponential rates that have again raised the question of the power of the internet.

What John Wesley didn't realize about his pioneering approach to church was that while most nineteenth-century church leaders exemplified what would be known as Sarnoff's Law, he exemplified Metcalfe's Law by establishing churches as nodes of spiritual growth and discourse rather than as just buildings where people meet. This is why one man, Wesley, with several hundred circuit riders in the nineteenth century, today boasts a staggering seventy-five million spiritual descendants in the United States alone — far more than anyone of his day ever could have imagined possible.[3]

We live in a time of potentially exponential growth for the church of Jesus Christ. As I mentioned in chapter 1, at no time in human history since the time of Genesis has more than 20 percent of the world's population been in direct contact with each other. Through the power of the virtual world, it is possible to create a church in which people from China, Korea, Japan, Russia, England, Germany, Brazil, Mexico, and the United States are active members. How can virtual churches leverage computer-mediated communication to create and become ministry nodes in a way that exponential kingdom growth can occur throughout our world?

Can a virtual church be a missional church? How will virtual churches engage in various forms of ministry? What types of virtual ministry will arise?

After the demise of Christendom in the West in the twentieth century, churches found themselves suddenly cut off from their privileged place in Western culture. This situation sparked a great deal of discussion about the purpose and nature of the church, with much more attention paid to ecclesiology than in previous eras. As we discussed in chapter 2, one of the more influential ecclesiologists of the twentieth century was Anglican Lesslie Newbigin, who held the church to be missional not just in activity but in purpose and nature. Newbigin's ideas are popular right now, especially among the mainline Protestant denominations hardest hit by their separation from temporal power.

As a Free Church pastor growing up on the cusp of the digital revolution, it seems to me the argument that a church must be missional is both valid and unnecessary. It is valid because from my tradition's viewpoint, ministry always should be a fundamental aspect of what it means to be the church. I would go so far as to argue that every church must be missional to be a real church, because voluntary association is not enough; the Spirit calls people together as the church to be, to go, and to do (and this doing we refer to in shorthand as ministry). There can be no doubt that ministry, the being and doing of church, was a part of the church at its inception.[4] Ministry is a natural and integrated function of the church.[5] In fact, in many cases it may be wise to try to understand the church by the ways it functions rather than by trying to discern the core of its intangible and esoteric nature.[6]

At the same time, the missional idea seems unnecessary, a reaction against a culturally sanctioned Christianity with which I am not totally familiar. A significant problem with stating that a church must be missional is the fact that the missional category is very broad and undefined.[7] When I read books by traditional church leaders in rapidly dying denominations calling for a missional approach, I wonder if they really understand what they are calling for, or if they are just trying to create a new program, template, or blueprint for their pastors to follow to stave off extinction. The missional idea is probably quite important for branches of the church that need reform, but how does the idea play for those churches that, for whatever reason, are largely uninfected by temporal power? How does the missional calling of the church affect virtual churches — churches that minister in a foreign world, churches for which Christendom has no effect and probably no meaning? Should virtual churches even speak of themselves as missional?

If people choose to speak of virtual churches as missional churches, it probably should not be as a reaction to Christendom; instead, it should be as a way to create a new DNA for the followers of Christ active in the virtual world. No matter the church tradition, Western churches in the real world struggle with the idea of church as a place, an organization, even a "spectator sport." While virtual churches have their issues, they probably could break the mold of the mundane way to do church in the West. If virtual churches can recover the basic idea of what it means to be the church, they can create churches in the virtual world based not around broadcast spectatorship but around engaged, participatory sponsorship of the cause of Christ (in both worlds).

A Participatory People

At the heart of any real church — regardless of the world in which it exists — must be people called by God to be his servants, proclaimers, apostles, and bridge builders to the world. Whether those people represent themselves in middle-class golf shirts and summer dresses, in coarse camel hair, or with 3D high-resolution avatars may not matter. What does matter is that they get involved, that they take hold of their calling to be ministers in their community. Can virtual churches encourage people to participate in ministry? Can they get

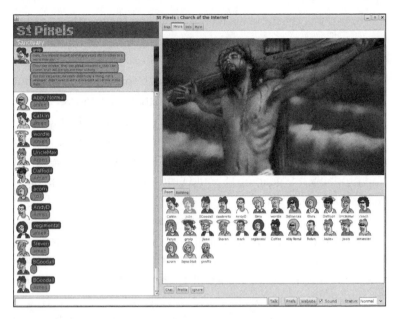

Worshipers participating in an Easter worship service at St. Pixels.

them to participate as much as in real-world churches? How about *more* than in real-world churches? Some virtual-church pastors to whom I have spoken believe this is possible. Will virtual churches, utilizing all of the power of computer-mediated communication, imbue Luther's idea of the priesthood of all believers with new life and new meaning?[8]

In Western culture, which is based on the cult of the individual, when Christians talk about the priesthood of all believers or the idea of "every member a minister," the philosophical heritage from Descartes to Kant to Locke kicks in and we visualize each Christian as a lone ministry-seeking missile that will singlehandedly engage our world. Many Christians worry that the virtual world and virtual churches will exacerbate this idea. Modern thinkers have given this homage to individualism euphemistic names such as "soul competency," but this image is a far cry from Luther and the church's original idea. Instead, the priesthood of all believers "has to do with our common responsibility to minister to one another and to the world" and not with any individual's right to "minister as he or she pleases."[9] I think we all can agree that people working together as the church is more powerful, more successful, than the effort of any one individual for the kingdom (1 Cor. 12:12 – 27).

The key to the church is its people being the church, being the agency of God in our world. Virtual churches seem to have the means to tap into the exponential power of the priesthood of all believers because of the highly connective nature of the virtual world. Think of it like this: every week at my real-world church, there are people who come in, sit in the seats, listen to the message, leave during the last song, and, at least from my vantage point, never do anything else. We could almost say that instead of their being the church, they are more Christendom's shadow remaining on the church in the Western world (James 2:17). Many of us attend churches where there are lots of people like that. With virtual churches (and we'll see this a lot more in the future when they better embrace the technology), there are ways to make all aspects of the church much more participatory. Virtual churches are already building on participatory ideas found on social networking sites such as MySpace and Facebook (which, like the church, don't work if people don't participate). How else can virtual churches increase participation and ministry? It seems to me that the more virtual churches move away from static broadcasts and implement some of the dynamics of virtual-world social networks, the more virtual churches will find that a much higher percentage of people will engage with and participate in their virtual church, leading to more ministry participation.[10] In fact, if the social-networking phenomenon is valid, virtual churches may find that some virtual churchgoers will become passionate or even overly enthusiastic about regular participation in their ministries. Will virtual churches change the way people participate in church? Will they change who participates, and how they participate?

Let me highlight two possibilities that I find very exciting.

First, I'm excited about virtual churches' ability to engage marginalized people in ministry. As a real-world pastor of a diverse multiethnic church in an urban, lower-middle class area of Northern California, I'm a realist, not an idealist. Many people who come to BVC come because life has been really tough for them, and they are finally at the point in their lives where they are willing to try God. Often these people struggle in ministry; it's a real challenge for them because their experiences show through and can make it really difficult to participate. Still, it's nothing less than awesome to see them engage their community for the gospel, knowing the "odds" are against them. The world would consider many of these people to be inconsequential or unimportant, but to God, they are each a cherished and highly valued part of the body of Christ.

In comparison, some of the virtual-church pastors I have spoken with have people in their churches who are *very* unimportant from the world's point of view. These churches have virtual churchgoers who are chronically shy, possess social phobias, have Tourette's syndrome, undergo deep internal struggles with gender, sexuality, racism, and many more issues, many of which make it difficult for them to integrate well into an average real-world church (much less serve in ministry).[11] Forget for a moment the question of whether the average real-world church could minister to an adult with Tourette's syndrome; would an adult with Tourette's syndrome even attempt to visit a real-world church? I suspect overcoming the fear would be quite difficult for many, especially since most "average" adults feel fear when they visit a new church for the first time. Can virtual churches reach these people? Can they reach people who would never go to a real-world church *because* the real-world church meets face-to-face?

What is the world's answer to these kinds of people? Eugenics? Abortion, for sure. Marginalization, definitely. Many real-world churches may try to reach these people, but as any pastor knows, it's not easy. Silicon Valley, where I live, has an extremely high percentage of people with autism; our church receives regular requests for help, but none of the people making these requests will ever come to our church. The number of people who live on the margins of our world — and of our class-stratified churches — is a lot larger than we think. However, in the virtual world, these people don't have to live on the margins, because at least at this point, there are no margins.[12] No one can judge them based on race, class, age, or handicap because the virtual world masks everyone as handsome robots (or some other avatar representation), greatly lowering the walls around the personal issues marginalized people face. For example, I know of one person who fully participates in a virtual church, even though this person struggles with the desire to dress as a member of the opposite sex.[13] Because this person is both a follower of Jesus and someone with a ministry-debilitating struggle, serving or even participating in a real-world church presents a challenge — for the person, the church, and all the people who attend the church. Serving in most ministries is probably out of the question; I doubt many suburban real-world pastors want a cross-dresser as a greeter at the front door every Sunday morning. Yet in this case, the person is able to participate in a virtual-world church and is even able to be open with the church's leadership team about their struggles and to receive godly support. They can even be a greeter!

What's so powerful about virtual churches' ability to engage marginalized people is that such people can actually participate in the ministry of the church in the virtual world, perhaps more so than they might be able to in the real world. Since they are telepresent with others, they don't have as many fears in the virtual world that handicap them in the real world. This is something that Descartes could not predict: people empowered to live not by their physical condition but by a calling much greater than themselves. As Christians, we can applaud any church — whether real or virtual — that cares about and reaches people on the margins.

Second, I'm excited about the virtual world's ability to teach people ministry skills in either virtual-world or real-world churches. One early big investor in the virtual world may seem strange to some — the United States military. For more than thirty years, the US military has been creating increasingly advanced virtual-world training scenarios. Military brass quickly saw the virtual world as an opportunity to save lives and limit damage by teaching their soldiers how to deal with crisis, hardship, and the toughest of situations before they encounter them in the "real world." The virtual world breaks down real-world walls and allows soldiers to understand the dynamics of their mission. Another investor is universities; just this year Imperial College London has started training med students in medical techniques in the virtual world that they can apply in future real-world situations. Can real-world churches use the virtual world to teach their ministry leaders how to deal with crisis and the toughest of situations before they encounter them in the real world? Can virtual-world churches leverage the virtual world to produce competent virtual-ministry leaders? If nothing else, virtual churches could equip people to minister and serve in a more controlled environment than the real world, some day transferring their skills into the real world.[14] No matter how you look at it, it's a win for the kingdom.

Imagine a person on the margins who struggles to participate in real-world churches because of the way they look, talk, or dress. Now imagine the freedom in Christ they have to fully participate in real, virtual-world churches. The person with the social phobia or debilitating handicap could become the avatar who is fearless about sharing the good news with others, tireless in their compassion for others, selfless in their help of others. Emboldened by their very real virtual-world experiences, this marginal person could grow in king-dom significance more and more both in the virtual world and in the real world as well.[15] What will the virtual world and virtual churches do for those with lesser handicaps? Can internet campuses engage a multitude of "average" people to become dedicated workers for the church and the kingdom? If they can overcome the big issue we'll talk about in the next chapter, virtual churches could be the most missional churches on earth.

Ministry by Immersion

If virtual churches can harness the power of fully participating people, can their ministries go viral? *Going viral* is a pop-culture term that describes a phenomenon that self-replicates and grows expo-nentially, like a virus. The term is often applied to elements of the virtual world such as videos and emails that affect (infect) users, and then those affected users send the content to other users, who also become affected. When users sense that viral content is malicious (in the case of viral marketing), they will try to avoid it, but when the content is benevolent (in the case of funny videos), they will promote it. Can virtual churches break the real-world mold of doing ministry and become fully immersed in the virtual world to create ministries that will affect millions of people for the cause of Christ?[16]

At its heart, ministry is not programs but the actions of people working in concert as a part of a local church. Right now, most virtual churches seem to have ministries that come straight from real-world churches. They have small groups, they have missions trips, they have counseling opportunities, and they have caregiv-ing sessions. Preliminary studies show that most traditional minis-tries such as these are as effective in the virtual world as they are in the real world.[17] We could talk about them, but as we've found, there really is very little difference between real-world and virtual-world churches — which is both a positive and a negative. Instead of reviewing ministries that are already employed, let's ask what virtual churches can do.

Before we do, virtual churches need to distinguish between ministry and marketing. I'm not antimarketing; I believe that marketing (or whatever you want to call it when churches use mass media to tell people about their church) can result in unchurched people coming to your church and considering the truth of the gospel. My real-world church is situated in a highly unchurched area of Northern California, and we use outreach strategies that some people would consider marketing. At the same time, I am not under the illusion that marketing is ministry. What's the difference between marketing and ministry in the virtual world? Just because a church creates funny videos or emails that go viral doesn't mean that church is engaged in a new type of virtual ministry. Far from it. In most cases, they are just employing virtual marketing strategies. How can virtual churches harness the mass-communication ability of the virtual world not just to market their church but to do actual ministry?

Virtual churches also need to distinguish between ministry and for-profit sales. Unfortunately, a great deal of Christian virtual space (especially if you count "ministry" websites) exists to hawk things from Jesus T-shirts to twenty-dollar sermon DVDs.[18] I'm not suggesting it's wrong to sell useful items at your virtual church. But let's be honest — in a lot of cases it's as much about making some extra coin to fund other ministries as it is about ministry itself. Remember the question we asked earlier: how do virtual churches improve their legitimacy? It seems to me one way is never to do anything in your virtual lobby (or website) that you would never do in the lobby of your real-world church. If real-world churches shouldn't look like the temple the hour before Jesus cleared it out, then neither should virtual churches. Somehow, pastors know that selling their sermon tapes in a real-world church is not exactly a ministry, but they seem to forget this when they sense the possibility of selling thousands of tapes online. We must remember that if the church exploits the virtual world, the virtual world will become that much harder to reach and that much more jaded, just as the real world has become today. How can virtual churches balance sales with doing ministry in the virtual world?

As virtual churches zero in on good ministry practices, they will be in a great position to unite the strengths of the virtual world with virtual church. They will be able to leverage technology to immerse the virtual world in works designed to bring people to Jesus. Early on, virtual churches recognized that they could bring evangelism to a whole new level in the virtual world. Discipleship ministries, counseling ministries, issues-based ministries, worship ministries, and fellowship ministries all seem to be a natural fit for virtual churches and may even play into the strengths of the virtual world. Let's apply the viral principle: given the power of computer-mediated communication, can these local, virtual-church ministries spread virally in such a way as to have a worldwide impact? Can virtual churches use viral techniques to minister to the whole world?

Consider this example: a real-world church can facilitate a support group for domestic violence survivors and it would be a great blessing for the people in that community, but its ministry is limited to the geographical reach of the church. Since a virtual church is not bound by geographical limits, it could facilitate the same support group in the virtual world, in a 3D environment created especially to facilitate healing and reach people around the globe. Meeting in the virtual world rather than in the real world presents quite a few advantages for survivors of abuse. Even more, the core of this group can not only reach out to other survivors from around the world but also easily transmit the contextualized truths they learn into the virtual world, affecting thousands, if not millions, of people.[19] Given this example, what's to stop virtual churches from greatly magnifying the power of ministry in both the real world and the virtual world?

Of course, to pull off viral, immersive ministries, virtual churches will need the same ministry vision, leadership, and communication abilities necessary to minister in the real world. If we consider all of the virtual churches spanning the virtual world right now, it seems to me that a high percentage of them are being led by pioneers — the kind of pioneers we see in movies who relocate to a new area, encounter a lot of problems, and eventually are run off their land. Weak pioneers. This is my assessment, but I base it on my observation of a wide range of virtual churches during a very fluid moment in time. This observation goes back to the assumption we talked about several chapters ago: anybody can start a virtual church with some virtual services or ministries. Perhaps this is the way it has always been for real-world churches, but for real, novel types of virtual ministry to occur, virtual churches need to develop strong yet humble, authoritative yet participatory avenues in which leadership can arise in the virtual world. In the end, virtual ministry, just like real-world ministry, will stand or fall on the vision, leadership, and communicative abilities of virtual churches.[20]

Finally, let's end this chapter on ministry with a challenge for virtual churches: how will they do ministries that appear to be impossible (or at a severe disadvantage) in the virtual world — ministries such as social, helps, or missions ministries? As we've seen, not only are real-world churches sending missionaries into the virtual world, but virtual churches are starting to send missionaries into the real world. Will virtual churches engage in social-justice ministries in the real world? Do they have any standing to do so? Since most of the virtual-ministry world is unexplored territory, it will remain to be seen how these types of ministries will work when they are started by virtual churches. It's not having every program under the sun that makes a church valid; rather, it's being missional that does. Can virtual churches be real churches without, for example, social ministries? Or will they redefine what it is to be social in the first place?

chapter 10

The Social-Network Church

As Hope's mother lay dying in a hospital bed, Hope came to me for help.

Hope is a woman in my real-world church, a woman who probably doesn't fit the middle-class mold, a person who probably is at the margins of other churches she previously attended. At BVC, she serves off and on in a variety of small ministries. She has many struggles, but I know she loves the Lord.

Like many people in San Jose, Hope was born outside of the United States, and most of her family speaks little or no English. They also have had little exposure to Christianity. Hope shared the gospel with her mother with no success until the week of her death. That week, as her mother lay in her hospital bed, she asked her daughter if a pastor could visit her to explain the gospel to her and, if all went well, baptize her. So Hope called me for help.

After Hope explained the situation over the phone, I was more than happy to go speak to her mother. There were two problems, though. First, her mother was in a hospital up in San Francisco. My mind immediately went to my schedule: could I fit this in? But realizing that I had to make this happen (as much as I hate driving to SF), I told Hope, "No problem. I'll go." The second problem was the deal breaker: I had forgotten that her mother spoke no English. When I suggested that Hope come with me to translate, she was very worried, in light of her mother's age and condition, that she and I would not be able to explain the gospel very clearly. She didn't want to take any chances with her mother's eternal destiny.

So I called several likeminded churches in San Francisco to see if one of them could send a pastor to visit this dying woman in her hospital bed. For the most part, these weren't blind calls; they were to churches whose pastors I had met or with whom I shared mutual friends.

None of those pastors or churches ever returned my calls or emails.

Hope also immediately started contacting friends who spoke her mother's language, and those friends contacted other friends, who contacted other friends, and the network grew up the peninsula from the South Bay to the North Bay. Within hours, Hope had lined up several pastors in Oakland and San Francisco to visit her mom.

I'm happy to report that Hope's mom accepted Jesus and was baptized in her hospital bed, the same one she died in the very next day.

I think we all know why Hope was successful at finding pastors who would help, while I, a pastor, could get no one to help, much less even email me back. In the church world, as in the real world, as in the virtual world, it's all about who you know.

Who you know is the "it" thing right now. Maybe it has always been that way, but the recent rise of social-networking sites has created a whole new understanding of the expression. Who's a friend on *your* Facebook, LinkedIn, or Twitter? Who are you connected with, and who do you know? What used to be an annual practice for young adults — having your friends sign your yearbook — has become a daily (if not hourly) practice for all adults: having your colleagues or friends write on your Facebook wall. People disconnected by geography are closer than ever via these developing social communities. The virtual world is radically transforming what it means to have friendships, to network, even to fellowship together.

 How will virtual churches build communities? Will they be global or local? What are the dangers associated with churches based on virtual social connectivity?

Virtual churches stand in line to complete and exponentially boost the idea of community fellowship through the power of shared, networked agency. When we look at the automobile, the automobile is an individualistic technology: individuals get into their cars and drive to church and drive to do ministry at a small group, an outdoor festival, a soup kitchen, or a community event. This type of technology culminated in the modern church. The virtual world is different from the automobile and the modern world. It exists and thrives only when people are in connection with each other.

What kinds of connections, though, will virtual churches form? We know small groups built solely on geography don't really work that well; small groups built on shared interests or needs work much better. Yet geography still matters because many people don't want to commute long distances to go to a small group, even one with shared interests. In real-world churches, what would small groups look like if you took geographical considerations off the table? Virtual churches eliminate geography, but does that mean that if we plant a virtual church, the world will come? John Wesley famously said that the world was his parish, but after the digital revolution, is this possible?[1] Or desirable?

Glocal Fellowships

Globalism is a hot topic, not just in politics but in the church as well. It seems as if everyone wants to go "glocal"—to be relevant not just in a local way but in a worldwide context. Pastors stream their sermons to the web and are excited that people in China appear to be watching them. Local churches in North America not only try to help the poor in their own neighborhoods but also raise money to fight AIDS in Africa. The church seems poised to be more global than ever, and virtual churches seem to be at the forefront.

In her sociological research of virtual churches, Heidi Campbell explains that many people take part in virtual churches because this participation makes them feel more connected to the church at large; a virtual church "provides the ability to extend their interactions with fellow believers and create a deeper awareness of what it means to be a part of the global Body of Christ."[2] She also explains that the feeling among many virtual-church attendees is that their real-world churches are limited in scope or viewpoint but that virtual-church participation contributes to greater global awareness. Yet we must ask, Is this perspective accurate? Are virtual churches an aggregate of global Christians, or are they much more localized than we might assume? Is the virtual world really as global as we think it is?

A growing body of evidence suggests that while the virtual world may be global in reach, it is local in association.[3] Let's consider our friends on Facebook, MySpace, or LinkedIn. How many friends do we have that live (or have lived) geographically close to us? Now let's count the number of friends we have from Papua New Guinea. How about Indonesia? Chile? China? Chances are that most of the people we know and will ever relate to—even through global systems such as social-networking sites and virtual worlds—are people who are related to us either through geography or strong common bonds such as interests, languages, hobbies, and goals. No matter how global the virtual world, most of our friends will be local to us (local in the sense of belonging to the same "neighborhood" or shared space as we discussed in chapter 3).

Is it really possible for virtual churches to be global churches? Should we as the church want them to be? The localizing nature of human association, coupled with the localizing nature of the church, suggests it very well may be impossible for any church truly to be a global church — at least not if it still wants to function as a truly local church. As we've discussed, a local church is a neighborhood of people together being the body of Christ. A local church is not just the closest religious building, but neither is it a random bunch of spectators from all over the world. Where people originate from doesn't matter; what matters is that they become a neighborhood for kingdom purposes. The glitch in creating a glocal church is that when the scope is so large, it's hard to see how healthy kingdom neighborhoods can be created.

We can see this in the area of proclamation; let's consider two examples. During the Church of Fools experiment, the Fools leadership team, based in the United Kingdom, invited guests to speak during their services. One of their speakers, a North American "celebulogian," spent the "sermon" talking about all of the problems with the current policies of the US government. Regardless of whether we agree with US policies, and laying aside the fact that this "sermon" didn't appear to have much to do with the gospel, how would this play for people in the US looking for spiritual fellowship at Church of Fools? If I preach against my perception of the policies of Vanuatu (an island nation in the South Pacific) in my real-world church, the only damage I do is to the people in my congregation who would have to listen to me. If I put it online, I risk offending a whole nation. Maybe Church of Fools didn't care about reaching people in the US with the gospel, but maybe it should have. Shouldn't it? Or should it instead try to reflect European values to reach Europeans with the gospel? Should a Christian church in Palestine speak against US policies if it will gain a hearing among secularized Palestinians? I'll be honest, I'm not much in favor of politics in church, but geopolitics opens up a box Pandora never could have imagined.[4]

Another, more innocent, example occurs at LifeChurch.tv services.[5] When I listen to Craig Groeschel or Perry Noble, who has substituted for Groeschel in the past, speak to their internet and Second Life campus, I often wonder who they perceive their audience to be. Especially Perry. Since I grew up in the rural South, I get the jokes about tractors, the Bible Belt language, and Americanisms. I can see LifeChurch.tv's messages striking a chord with *local* people — and by that I don't mean people in Oklahoma; I mean people who appreciate tractors, all-American superheroes, and these sorts of things. These messages may appeal to local people such as a farmer in Georgia or a sheepherder in Georgia (the *other* one), but what about savvy DINKs in Tulsa (especially in light of the fact that the US is now more urban than rural)? Is it even possible for virtual churches to proclaim the gospel in a way that would, at the same time, be meaningful to a politician in Managua, a businesswoman in Kuala Lumpur, and a teenager in Quebec? Does God intend for it to work like that? Or is it for this very reason that he tells us to "love your neighbor" instead of to "love your world" (Matt. 22:39)?[6] Should we proclaim a vanilla gospel to the world, or a rum-raisin gospel to a targeted group of people? (Do church leaders in South Korea or Vanuatu who are interested in virtual churches know what rum raisin is?)

The virtual world is not really a global village. Patricia Wallace explains that "with respect to human interaction, it is more like a huge collection of distinct neighborhoods where people with common interests can share information, work together, tell stories, joke around, debate politics, help each other out, or play games."[7] Will these virtual neighborhoods be the foundation for healthy churches, or segregated Christian clubs?

The Church as Guild

Sociologists and ethnographers are very interested in the rise of the virtual world because of what it reveals about the nature of people, groups, and communities. When MMORPGs such as World of Warcraft exploded in population, with people from all over the world playing, something very interesting took place. It did become a melting pot

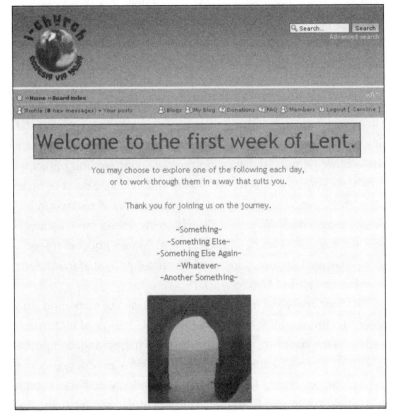

An i-church virtual connection point for Lent.

in the sense that people from all over the world played together and competed with each other, but not in the sense that these people formed global communities. Instead, what happened is that most of the millions of people grouped themselves into guilds — small, tight communities with shared goals for the game or shared interests. These guilds were not global; even though some had players from several different countries (not the norm), they were localized clans that roved the Warcraft countryside. Warfare is often fought not one-on-one or civilization-against-civilization but guild-against-guild, clan-against-clan. When someone from another clan kills one of your clan members, you go after one of their clan members.

While it may be news to people who don't take part in a church or civic organization, we who are committed to a local church intuitively know that people like to group themselves into guilds (clans, cliques, gangs). We've all been to that church where roving guilds (we like to call them committees in Baptist churches) war with other guilds (maybe you call them boards) for gain or for control. Is this the kind of church we want to unite with, to minister to? No. Even while some people are heralding the decentralized and participatory power of the virtual world, history and evidence don't seem to be in their favor. There's a great danger that the virtual world will simply spawn packs of roving church guilds united more by ideology and interests than by gospel mission. Can we fight what seems to be inherent human nature to group ourselves by shared interests or common culture? Should we?

The modern world introduced us to the idea of marketing, and recent technology has really sharpened the power of niche marketing. In the near future, if it's not already happening, computer-mediated communication (and globalism) will allow every product to be niche marketed.[8] Traditional church leaders who hated church marketing at the end of the twentieth century haven't seen anything; just wait till they see what happens when churches begin to harness the virtual world to niche market the gospel to a global population. If we take the lesson learned over the last few decades to heart, it's that every church markets itself to some demographic, even if it never does anything outreach-oriented and is vehemently opposed to church marketing; whether it realizes it or not, its marketing demographic is inward-looking curmudgeons. Real-world churches use niche marketing, but there's a difference between marketing a real-world church and marketing a virtual-world church.

In the words of one blogger, "The church is shifting from a central meeting place of a widely diverse human community united by geography, to a dispersed meeting place for those of relatively similar [interest-based] aims."[9] If this comes to fruition, it could be a very bad day for the church at large: the church becomes a club. In the real world, there is no doubt that most people pick churches based on the popularity of the pastor, on who they know who attends the church, on shared interests, or on what they believe they can get out of the church — or worse, on race and class. We all recognize that none of these are ideal. At the same time, geography does limit these tendencies; if someone moves to a new area and looks for a good, Bible-teaching church, and their only options are one church five minutes away comprised mostly of people of a different race and class and with different interests, and one an hour away that is comprised of people similar to themselves, where would this person choose to worship? We could debate this. Cynically, I expect more would make the hour-long drive to worship with people like them, but geography does often force diverse people to worship together. This diversity is a strength of the church, not a weakness. I don't say this because of some sociopolitical ideology; I say this because the Bible tells us that the body of Christ has a diverse membership (1 Cor. 12:12 – 13). We may all agree that "the church is not to be held together by social bonds such as being of the same race or class or income, but by the spiritual bond of a common possession of the Holy Spirit" (see also Gal. 3:28).[10]

There is a real danger that virtual churches, perhaps by their presence or perhaps intentionally, will niche market to people who are exactly like themselves, creating guilds of Christians built around narrow ideologies. I could not create and sustain a real-world church that requires attendees to affirm and live out a ninety-point statement on every gray area of Christian faith, but the global reach of the virtual world makes such a church possible. While geography forces some degree of heterogeneity, the virtual world strongly encourages ideological homogeneity. Recently I attended a rapidly growing church-plant that has attracted some national media attention and was supposed to be a "new way of doing church," but I couldn't help noticing that every person at that service (except for me and the senior pastor) was Caucasian, twentysomething, pierced, and tattooed with spiky hair.[11] In the virtual world, churches could become far more segregated than they already are in the real world — interest-based guilds or echo chambers for obscurantist ideologies, not healthy, missional bodies of Christ.[12] Perhaps this is truer of blogs and some text-based types of virtual churches, but the danger remains for all. Church shopping can take on a whole new meaning with the proliferation of virtual churches.

Accessing Church

Other factors limit the global reach of virtual churches. A major one is language. I'll be honest, I had a hard time tracking down virtual churches that don't use English. While they're not as prevalent or well-known as some English-language ones, they're out there. How can a virtual church be a global church if the language of proclamation is only English?[13] It can reach only the most educated, or perhaps the most world-savvy, in other cultures. Bill Chastain, pastor of Church of the Simple Faith and an early virtual-church pioneer, translated his text-based services into other languages only to find that native speakers of those languages contacted him for more conversational renderings. As we can see, culture also plays a big part; my inability to find many examples of virtual churches outside of North America and Western Europe may reflect less of a language gap than a culture gap. Finally, of course, there is the problem that virtual churches can reach only people who have internet access. While the number of people with access will continue to skyrocket in the years ahead, there will always be a technological barrier between the haves and the have nots.[14] To a certain degree, lack of access stands against the very nature of the gospel — a good news, radically inclusive, for all people.

There are also ways in which virtual churches will make access to the gospel much easier. As we touched on earlier, the fact that virtual churches can meet at any time and that anyone can access them at any computer terminal creates a whole new missional scenario.[15] People who lack the blessing of their society, government, or family to attend a real-world church now may have unfettered access to a real church, just one in the virtual world. The desire to grow in faith in Jesus Christ is more powerful than any organizational scheme or personal interest, and challenges all believers to access and fully participate in the church.[16] While we can say that a virtual church is in many ways more local than global, is it accessible to all people, or only certain segments of people?

Reaching SimFamilies

Critics see virtual churches as promoting isolationism and individualism and contributing to the destruction and fragmentation of the traditional family as more and more adults log on to private computer terminals to attend church and worship alone. Some virtual churches in Second Life even planted their churches in adults-only areas, preventing access to anyone under eighteen. According to critics and conventional wisdom, virtual churches are destined to allow access primarily to single adults, business travelers, home-bound individuals, soldiers in the field, and other people in individualistic contexts. Clearly, limiting access doesn't seem very healthy. Is there a way for virtual churches to reach more than just individuals, to reach the fundamental unit of people, the family?

I believe the answer is yes. I believe virtual churches have the potential to reach families just as well as, and maybe in some ways more effectively than, real-world churches. I know, I know, you think I'm crazy. Let's hash it out.

The most important ingredient in any society is the family. If there were a real-world church that excluded families, it probably wouldn't last that long. Right now, virtual churches are stuck in a situation that excludes families from participating, greatly limiting their accessibility to the average person. Let me say it another way: people are not flocking to virtual churches in the way that they would if virtual churches were accessible to the whole family. In my conversations with virtual-church pastors, this is a technological limitation, not a ministry conviction. Virtual-church pastors want to reach families, not just individuals, but current technology prevents this from happening in 2008.[17] Still, we're at the beginning of the digital revolution, not the end. In the Western world, most people will soon possess computer-connected television monitors or projectors so large they will feel fully immersed in what they watch on them — large enough that a family could project a virtual service on the wall of their home and all take part as a family. It's weird, because virtual churches might represent a return to a *traditional* type of church. Instead of the modern situation in which the family gets up, gets ready, travels an hour in an automobile to go to church with people like themselves, and, when they arrive, splits up to worship individually in specialized ministry areas, families will get up, sit around in their pj's eating breakfast, turn on the monitor connecting them to their virtual church, and worship in perhaps the most family-friendly environment the world has ever known.

Some of you may feel like my example of family virtual worship is like a scene out of *The Jetsons*, so let me offer one example that can happen today. One powerful form of witness is corporate worship, but we all know that many nonbelievers won't go to church in the real world to explore this for themselves. We all know how much easier it is to invite people over to our homes than to our churches — that's the beauty of small groups. What if future, virtual-world-based small groups were more powerful than today's small groups because they are full-on worship experiences? What if we invite our friends over to our house not just for nachos and chili-cheese fries and some discussion but to participate in a virtual-church worship service — especially one that is able to harness the power of the virtual world to allow for attendee participation? What if a virtual-church pastor spoke to hundreds of these "worship parties" around the real world? What if leveraging technology actually put the church on the growth pattern of Reed's Law?

Against all odds, the church was thriving.

Hermas was never one to fault success, and as unlikely as it seemed, the church in Iconium was not just growing; it was thriving. He hated to admit it, but the growth was a little bit exciting.

It seemed like a long time ago, more than eight years to be exact, since Hermas became a follower of the Way. He had been at Sylvus' house after church, listening to a discussion between several foreign Jews and the leaders of the Iconium church about the struggle between imperial politics and Jews who rejected the Way. The now-common occurrence of foreign Jews passing through the city hadn't bothered Hermas, but the conversation did.

Hermas was the last one in his family to get baptized; Rhoda and their children were immersed two years before he was in the local stream that watered the orchards. That day had held more meaning for Hermas than he realized at the time.

About four years ago, things starting changing for the church at Sylvus' house. Not only did it continue to grow, with new churches starting all over the city, but leaders from other churches — not just wandering prophets — began to visit. They brought with them testimonies of the disciples who first followed Jesus, and letters that clarified positions and practices of the church. At Sylvus' house, many of these letters and testimonies were thoroughly debated and discussed; in the proper Jewish manner, there was a great amount of vigor put into the working out of Jesus' message. Hermas even took part at times.[a]

The world was changing, and the church, the Way, was changing it. Hermas may have been uncomfortable with this when he was younger, but he had changed too. Now he was cautiously optimistic about it — at least until the Messiah returned, as he had promised.

In his heart, Hermas knew that amid all the criticism and wrangling about the church, the church had an answer people needed. From his perspective, the church possessed a hope that would change the world.

---

a. A great reference work on the development of the message of the early church is Birger Gerhardsson, *Memory and Manuscript: Oral Tradition and Written Transmission in Rabbinic Judaism and Early Christianity; with "Tradition and Transmission in Early Christianity"* (Grand Rapids, Mich.: Eerdmans, 1998).

Conclusion

A Church on Every Node

What is the future of virtual churches?

In the twenty-first century, what will the church be? What will the church do? Will it stay rooted in the forms of the twentieth century? The eighteenth century? The sixteenth century? The twelfth century? Or will it move forward and embrace new ways of being the church? In the twentieth century, a local church could not really reach the whole world, but in the twenty-first century, virtual churches will have that kind of reach.

Will virtual churches open up the gospel to all people? What will virtual churches teach us about the nature of being the church?

What will the growth of virtual churches reveal to us about church itself? About being fully devoted followers of Jesus in a variety of different worlds?

All Your Base Are Belong to Us

Today is the third most exciting time to be alive in Christian history; we're on the cusp of the third wave of the church. Only three times in history have technological breakthroughs plus explosive population movements equaled massive transformation in the people of God. The first was in the first century AD. The church was a new expression of the people of God after the coming of the Messiah. The technological marvel of the Roman road system coupled with the continuing proliferation of the written word allowed the early church to spread the gospel and plant new churches more rapidly and more effectively than it could have at any other time prior to that. The second was in the sixteenth century. The church desperately needed reform. The invention of the printing press and the awakening of the mind in Europe contributed to an explosion of the church, and a way of doing church, that we still feel to this very day. The third wave will be in the twenty-first century. The church will enter new worlds to proclaim the gospel to the nations. The rise of computer-mediated communication, globalism, and projected population booms worldwide will propel the church to find new ways to be the church. These new ways, one of which will be virtual churches, will affect the way we become the church for several centuries to come.

What if virtual churches transform the way we do church and what it means for us to be the church?[19] Throughout this book, we discussed the virtual world without making any specific predictions about its future, but we must not be misled to believe that the internet of today will be the same thing as the virtual world of tomorrow. Just think about where technology was ten years ago. Email was new for most people; the internet was text-based and low-resolution, and it took forever to locate anything using dial-up connections. Where will the internet, the virtual world, be in ten years? Twenty years? I don't have any idea. I'll leave that up to the people who predict flying cars and moonbases. But we can be certain of two things:

first, the virtual world will be very different, and second, the church must start now—immediately—if it wants to be a significant part of the virtual world in the future. In the United States, the church has been playing catch-up in areas such as music and film for most of the second half of the twentieth century because it foolishly wasted God-given opportunities to engage those media in the first half of the twentieth century. The question is, Will the church at large learn from these mistakes? Or repeat them?

What if virtual churches change our real-world landscape? The real-world church I pastor in San Jose is on a tiny piece of land that no church plant could ever afford to buy today. Rapid urbanization means that buying land will be increasingly difficult for most new church plants.[20] Virtual churches can create worship spaces at a tiny fraction of the cost of planting churches in the real world, and virtual churches will never run out of room.[21] What if virtual churches combine the best of the virtual world and the best of the real world in one scalable package? What if it played out like this: virtual-church planters will plant a church in the virtual world and, instead of focusing on a mythical global congregation, target mostly an urban geographic area. In this area, they will set up first tens, then hundreds, of virtual-church nodes—homes with projection systems (which certainly will become less expensive in a few years) that are transformed into micro worship centers where people invite more people to take part in local, corporate virtual worship and discipleship. These churches will see the computer not as a terminal or an end point but as a site or node or hub where a small group can gather. In this situation, wouldn't such a virtual church become the ultimate multisite church as it is empowered to have not just three or four sites, but hundreds, if not thousands, of sites in one area or, for a few virtual churches, all around the world?

I believe virtual churches will never replace real-world churches,[22] and I believe they shouldn't, because both are real churches—just in different worlds with different ministry practices and strategies — united by the presence of Christ and his Spirit guiding both forms of church. It seems to me that real-world churches will accomplish ministry objectives that virtual-world churches and internet campuses will struggle to accomplish, just as virtual-world churches and internet campuses will accomplish ministry objectives that real-world churches will struggle to accomplish.[23] What if in the future (maybe not immediately but soon), most people don't see virtual churches as a form of church different from real-world churches? What if they see both as just churches? If this happens, it will occur all the more rapidly as real-world churches adopt more and more virtual elements, and as virtual churches create real-world ministry teams that reach people in the real world as well as in the virtual world. I also believe that the more each type of church steps into the other type's world, the more unity and cooperation there will be. If I had to make one flying-car type of speculation, it'd be this: by the twenty-second century, every real-world church will be partially virtual-world, and every virtual-world church will be partially real-world. It'll be a great win for the church of Christ.

The advent of virtual churches is creating a compelling side effect: for the first time in several centuries, the church is faced with a new form of church. What will this brand-new form teach the church as a whole about being the church? Will it skewer unfounded presuppositions? Will it sharpen our understanding of ministry and practice? Will it help unify disparate groups of churches who hold the same basic theology? Yes, it can do all of this, and more. As I wrote this book, I learned a little bit about virtual ministry but a whole lot about the nature of the church itself. Nearly everyone I spoke to in private conversation felt the same way — virtual churches constructively challenge our view of church, for the better.[24] When you get right down to it, in most ways there is little difference between being the church in the virtual world and being the church in the real world. The geography may be different, but the church is still the church no matter where it is found.

Paul Minear makes two important observations in his book *Images of the Church in the New Testament* that are relevant here. First is the fact that the church in the New Testament writings is always presented as an image, an idea, a possibility, or a hope.[25] Anytime people try to create organizations, bylaws, or precedents to create a church, it always is destined to fall short of God's plan. Second is the realization that the apostle Paul never speaks of the distinction between synagogue and church, old Israel and new Israel. For Paul, there is only one Israel, only one church.[26] Virtual churches are real expressions of the church and are a part of the church at large — just one image, one idea, one possibility, one hope of the way real church might be.

A Call to Apostolic Digerati

Twelve years before the writing of this book, Patrick Dixon predicted in his book *Cyberchurch* that the number of virtual Christian ministries would explode, but that hasn't happened.[27] Sure, the number of real-world churches with websites has exploded, but websites don't reach people any more than billboards do. They're great for advertising but ineffective for fostering changed lives. Let me be clear: Dixon is not the one who was wrong; the church was. The church at large is already behind the technological curve. The best opportunity for the church in the twenty-first century is to engage technology — and people — head on.[28]

All over our world, there are young men and women who were born after the start of the digital revolution, who have no memory of the agrarian and industrial eras. They know only the digital world. The church must find these people. The church must raise up new pioneers, apostolic digerati who are willing to partner with experienced pastors and church leaders to truly engage the virtual world. Apostolic digerati are not just people who are interested in technology; they are people to whom God has given a talent for technological innovation and the heart of an apostle. Just as the church in ages past needed masons, architects, and artists to create spaces where people could feel prepared to worship God, so too does the church today need coders and futurists with contrite hearts to build new types of churches for new types of people. If that's you, now's the time; the virtual world is the place. To reach the virtual world, the church must ask God to send new apostles for a new generation and a new way of doing church.

I didn't write this book to be a "part of the conversation" or to claim that my way of doing church is better than your way because I have more people, money, and fame. I didn't write it to tear down other people's views of church, which unfortunately has always been a popular aim. My singular intent and hope is to build up the church by encouraging people to invest in people who inhabit virtual worlds. Should every church open up an internet campus? Should many churches create a Second Life campus or small group? Should all pastors get on Facebook or Twitter to their people? What if some brave apostolic digerati in the near future created an open-source, 3D worship environment (a la the Church of Fools experiment) that any church could easily adapt to their own style of service? These are the kinds of questions we need to be asking now, if not yesterday.

Mark Brown at Anglican Cathedral impresses on us that the virtual world is "a new mission field. We are called by God to pitch our tent in this strange land and learn the language, so that we can share God's love."[29] Pitching our tent doesn't mean posting websites or podcasting sermons; it means dwelling with people in that place. The only way to dwell in meaningful relationships with people in the virtual world is to create community, to plant virtual churches. God calls the church to be "an adventurous colony in a society of unbelief."[30] We ask God for adventurous colonies in a virtual world of unbelief. May God prepare the harvest, and may the workers — the virtual pioneers — not be few.

Recommended Reading

Boellstorff, Tom. *Coming of Age in Second Life: An Anthropologist Explores the Virtually Human*. Princeton, N.J.: Princeton University Press, 2008.

Brasher, Brenda E. *Give Me That Online Religion*. San Francisco: Jossey-Bass, 2001.

Campbell, Heidi. *Exploring Religious Community Online: We Are One in the Network*. Digital Formations 24. New York: Peter Lang, 2005.

Cooper, Robbie. *Alter Ego: Avatars and Their Creators*. London: Boot, 2007.

Guest, Tim. *Second Lives: A Journey through Virtual Worlds*. New York: Random House, 2007.

Küng, Hans. *The Church*. New York: Sheed and Ward, 1967.

Minear, Paul S. *Images of the Church in the New Testament*. New Testament Library. Louisville: Westminster John Knox, 2004.

Palfrey, John, and Urs Gasser. *Born Digital: Understanding the First Generation of Digital Natives*. New York: Basic, 2008.

Smart, John, Jamais Cascio, and Jerry Paffendorf. "Metaverse Roadmap: Pathways to the 3D Web: A Cross-Industry Public Foresight Project." Unpublished paper, 2007.

Solove, Daniel J. *The Future of Reputation: Gossip, Rumor, and Privacy on the Internet*. New Haven, Conn.: Yale University Press, 2007.

Notes

Preface

1. For example, one digitopian claims the internet will cause people to start thinking as ancient Hebrews did (Thomas Hohstadt, "The Geeks of the Gospel: Sorcerer's Apprentice or Empowered Prophet?" in *Voices of the Virtual World: Participative Technology and the Ecclesial Revolution*, ed. Leonard Hjalmarson and John La Grou [Wikiklesia, 2007], 119); one alarmist rants about everything from the evils of internet churches to "the strange powers of word processing" (Douglas Groothuis, *The Soul in Cyberspace* [Grand Rapids, Mich.: Baker, 1997], 65).
2. Nicholas M. Healy, *Church, World and the Christian Life: Practical-Prophetic Ecclesiology* (Cambridge: Cambridge University Press, 2000), 31.
3. Ibid., 6; and see also John S. Hammett, *Biblical Foundations for Baptist Churches: A Contemporary Ecclesiology* (Grand Rapids, Mich.: Kregel, 2005), 20.
4. Hans Küng, *The Church* (New York: Sheed and Ward, 1967), 19.

Chapter 1: Church in the Virtual World

1. Throughout this book, I will use the word *modern* in its most common usage, as a description of the world from the time of the Enlightenment until today. The few instances in which I use the term as a demarcation point against postmodernism will be clear from the context.
2. As with the internet, there has always been debate about who invented the radio, largely because of the power and complexity of the invention.
3. Paul Twomey, "Keynote Speech: ITU/MII Seminar on Internet Development on Online Environment" (Zhengzhou, China, October 11, 2006).
4. Ibid.
5. This estimate is based on financial data acquired from SEC filings of the largest bookstores in the United States.
6. A blog (weblog) is self-published textual content; a wiki is a website or virtual world built by a "hive" or collective societal minds; a MMOG is a "massively multiplayer online game," in which thousands of people all over the world play together in real time in a virtual world.

7. Estimate based on a typical media item sold on websites such as eBay or Amazon.

8. Throughout this book, I will refer to the various "waves" of the evolution of the internet (from an "average Joe" perspective). The first wave includes early features such as text-only email, internet browsers, and instant messaging. The second wave includes applications that are multiperson interactive or allow for the manipulation and development of publishable content. Future waves, which have not yet arrived, will include anything beyond the first two waves, such as voice-to-voice imaging protocols, 3D immersive and simulative environments, and stimulation of more than two senses. I use these descriptions as simple categories only.

9. Brenda E. Brasher, *Give Me That Online Religion* (San Francisco: Jossey-Bass, 2001), 23.

10. A great example is the University of Phoenix, a virtual university.

11. There is some debate over whether the virtual world is more of a medium or a place, but since I tend to feel it is both, for the remainder of this book I will use both ideas interchangeably to describe the virtual world.

12. Tim Guest, *Second Lives: A Journey through Virtual Worlds* (New York: Random House, 2007), 6.

13. To put it in perspective, seventy million people is the population of France. The number of people concurrently playing games in virtual worlds is already larger than the population of Singapore; see Leo Sang-Min Whang and Geunyoung Chang, "Lifestyles of Virtual World Residents: Living in the On-Line Game 'Lineage,'" *CyberPsychology and Behavior* 7:5 (2004): 593.

14. All of the virtual-world inhabitants I interviewed for this book had seasons in their lives when they spent at least forty hours per week in virtual worlds.

15. LifeChurch.tv measures attendance by the number of IP addresses logged on. While a logged IP address might be a sleeper (someone who logged on but did not participate), it also might be that more than one person was gathered around a single computer during the worship experience.

16. Tim Hutchings, "Creating Church Online: A Case-Study Approach to Religious Experience," *Studies in World Christianity* 13:3 (2007): 245.

17. As of the writing of this book, the original Church of Fools is now a chapel for individuals, but some of the creators have started a new virtual church, St. Pixels.

18. Americans are in the minority in virtual worlds (see Guest, *Second Lives*, 27). I am humbled by the fact that our European and Asian-Oceanic brothers and sisters are way out in front of the US church in virtual-church planting.

19. Before disagreeing with this argument, remember that many of us have already been at least partially assimilated into the postmodern era and to a certain degree think as postmoderns do. We have to consider the way moderns thought and behaved sixty years ago.

20. It is impossible to give a complete explanation here for postmodernism or to defend its rationality. See, for example, Heath White's *Postmodernism 101: A First Course for the Curious Christian* (Grand Rapids, Mich.: Brazos, 2006).

21. Bill, a twenty-one-year-old high-school graduate from Seattle and assistant manager of a fast food restaurant, is an avid MMOG (massively multiplayer online game) player. Many of his closest relationships were formed online or as a result of the MMOG.

22. Simon Jenkins, interviewed in Tim Hutchings, "Theology and the Online Church," *Epworth Review* 35:1 (2008).

Chapter 2: The Cyber-Driven Church

1. There are several different arguments here. One is presented by Douglas Groothuis, a professor of religion at Denver Seminary, who argues that the virtual world is both real and unreal, depending on the situation (Douglas Groothuis, *The Soul in Cyberspace* [Grand Rapids, Mich.: Baker, 1997], 85 and 25, respectively). Another is presented by Jonathan Tobias, who believes that since the virtual world is an incomplete world, it can't be real (Jonathan Tobias, "No Life in Second Life: Orthodoxy's Problem with Virtual Reality," *Again* 29:3 [2007]). However, both of these arguments confuse phenomenology with ontology and therefore fail to hold any "real" water.

2. For example, see Heidi Campbell, "Congregation of the Disembodied: A Look at Religious Community on the Internet," in *Virtual Morality: Morals, Ethics, and New Media*, ed. Mark J. P. Wolf (New York: Peter Lang, 2003), 196.

3. Rather than a fictional world or a purely imaginary world, for example.

4. Neil Ormerod, "The Structure of a Systematic Ecclesiology," *Theological Studies* 63:1 (2002): 3.

5. John G. Stackhouse Jr., ed., *Evangelical Ecclesiology: Reality or Illusion?* (Grand Rapids, Mich.: Baker, 2003), 9.

6. Nicholas M. Healy, *Church, World and the Christian Life: Practical-Prophetic Ecclesiology* (Cambridge: Cambridge University Press, 2000), 2.

7. Hans Küng, *The Church* (New York: Sheed and Ward, 1967), 4. This is echoed by Andrew Careaga, *eMinistry: Connecting with the Net Generation* (Grand Rapids, Mich.: Kregel, 2001), 19.

8. In light of the fluid discussion, my categories simply represent broad areas of thought and are not always indicative of every nuance of the views of each of the people cited.

9. For example, Groothuis calls virtual churches a "transparent folly," and those who promote virtual churches are "insidious" (Groothuis, *The Soul in Cyberspace*, 159). *Luddite* was a pejorative term for early-nineteenth-century English workers who protested new technology by destroying it. A neo-Luddite is a modern person who is against change through technology.

10. For example, Patrick Dixon, *Cyberchurch: Christianity and the Internet* (Eastbourne, UK: Kingsway, 1997), 157; John S. Hammett and Jonathan Merritt, "Surfing the Church? Can Real Connection Be Found Online?" *Relevant Leader* (2008): 42–46; and possibly Scot McKnight, a professor of theology at North Park University, based on discussion with the author on July 2008.

11. For example, John Hammett, in discussion with the author, July 2008.

12. For example, Heidi Campbell, a professor of communication at Texas A&M University, studied several online religious communities and concluded that most people view these communities (which include virtual churches) as supplemental to real-world faith communities; see Heidi Campbell, *Exploring Religious Community Online: We Are One in the Network*, Digital Formations 24 (New York: Peter Lang, 2005), 191; and also Calvin Park, "Using the Machine," in *Voices of the Virtual World: Participative Technology and the Ecclesial Revolution*, ed. Leonard Hjalmarson and John La Grou (Wikiklesia, 2007), 242–44.

13. For example, Tom Beaudoin, *Virtual Faith: The Irreverent Spiritual Quest of Generation X* (San Francisco: Jossey-Bass, 1998), 88; Bobby Gruenewald, innovation pastor of LifeChurch.tv, in discussion with the author, August 2008; Pam Smith, priest in charge of i-church, in discussion with the author, August 2008; Mark Brown, priest in charge of the Anglican Cathedral in Second Life, in discussion with the author, July 2008; Troy Gramling, lead pastor of Flamingo Road Church, in discussion with the author, November 2008; and Brian Vasil, internet campus pastor of Flamingo Road Church, in discussion with the author, September 2008.

14. We continue to use the word *church* today by convention.

15. Everett Ferguson, *The Church of Christ: A Biblical Ecclesiology for Today* (Grand Rapids, Mich.: Eerdmans, 1996), 130; see also D. A. Carson, *Exegetical Fallacies*, 2nd ed. (Grand Rapids, Mich.: Baker, 1996), 28–33.

16. Paul Minear's classic study lists ninety-six different metaphors; see Paul S. Minear, *Images of the Church in the New Testament*, New Testament Library (Louisville: Westminster John Knox, 2004).

17. Avery Dulles, *Models of the Church*, expanded ed. (New York: Doubleday, 1987), 206.

18. Campbell, "Congregation of the Disembodied," 180.

19. John S. Hammett, *Biblical Foundations for Baptist Churches: A Contemporary Ecclesiology* (Grand Rapids, Mich.: Kregel, 2005), 31.

20. In an article criticizing the validity of virtual churches, John Hammett and Jonathan Merritt contend that most virtual-church proponents emphasize the universal church over the local church. In this chapter, I argue the opposite, that a virtual church is just another type of local church. What is more, most opponents of the virtual church emphasize the ideal church rather than the fallible church, a position heavily criticized by Karl Barth,

Hans Küng, Nicholas Healy, and others; see Hammett and Merritt, "Surfing the Church?" 42 – 46.

21. Miroslav Volf, a professor of theology at Fuller Seminary, explains that even though Matthew 18:20 is often quoted by Free Church advocates (such as myself) in discussions about the church, the verse does have a prestigious history of usage in discussions about the church throughout church history; see Miroslav Volf, *After Our Likeness: The Church as the Image of the Trinity*, Sacra Doctrina (Grand Rapids, Mich.: Eerdmans, 1998), 135 – 36.

22. Donald A. Hagner, *Matthew 14 – 28*, Word Biblical Commentary 33B (Dallas: Word, 1995), 533 – 34; and Craig S. Keener, *A Commentary on the Gospel of Matthew* (Grand Rapids, Mich.: Eerdmans, 1999), 455 – 56.

23. Hendrikus Boers, *Neither on This Mountain nor in Jerusalem: A Study of John 4*, SBLMS 35 (Atlanta: Scholars, 1988), 176.

24. Andreas J. Köstenberger, *John*, Exegetical Commentary on the New Testament (Grand Rapids, Mich.: Baker, 2004), 153.

25. Augustine, *Tractates on the Gospel of John 11 – 27*, trans. John W. Rettig (Washington, D.C.: Catholic University of America, 1988), 93.

26. W. D. Davies, *The Gospel and the Land: Early Christianity and Jewish Territorial Doctrine* (Berkeley: University of California Press, 1974), 336; and Köstenberger, *John*, 157 – 59.

27. Notably, Jesus responds to the Samaritan woman in the plural form of *you*, meaning "all you people."

28. In the original language, "in" is used to locate all three "places" of worship: in the (Samaritan) mountain, in Jerusalem, and in the Spirit. This usage represents a blunter form of the language — it's not designed to be understood metaphorically or metaphysically. You could almost say the Spirit is the place of worship.

29. Ormerod, "The Structure of a Systematic Ecclesiology," 5; and Roger Haight, *Christian Community in History: Historical Ecclesiology* (New York: Continuum, 2004), 42.

30. Signs and wonders in a literal manner as the book of Acts means the expression, not hype or blind faith.

31. We'll discuss the issue of community more in chapters 3 and 9.

32. Hammett, *Biblical Foundations for Baptist Churches*, 44 – 45; and Küng, *The Church*, 171.

33. Andrew Careaga, *eMinistry: Connecting with the Net Generation* (Grand Rapids, Mich.: Kregel, 2001), 55.

34. We'll take up the issue of locality in the next chapter.

35. The NIV and other translations render Paul's joining with the church "in spirit," but a better case can probably be made that Paul means "in the Holy Spirit"; see Anthony C. Thiselton, *The First Epistle to the Corinthians: A Commentary on the Greek Text* (Grand Rapids, Mich.: Eerdmans, 2000), 391.

36. Some may wonder whether Paul was taking on himself the authority of bishop, allowing him to be absent but still a part of these local churches.

Such a theory may be anachronistic, but even if it were true, it would bolster the virtual church's argument for being a valid church in the area of ordinances or sacraments. We'll take this up in chapter 5.

37. Whether in the real world or the virtual world, space and geography can limit different types of human agency, and there are different limits in different worlds.

38. Minear, *Images of the Church in the New Testament*, 225.

39. Wolfhart Pannenberg, *Systematic Theology*, trans. Geoffrey W. Bromiley (Grand Rapids, Mich.: Eerdmans, 1998), 3:20; and Peter L'Huillier, "Ecclesiology in the Canons of the First Nicene Council," *St. Vladimir's Theological Quarterly* 27:2 (1983): 119.

40. Nicholas Healy, "Ecclesiology and Communion," *Perspectives in Religious Studies* 31:3 (2004): 276.

41. Wilhelm Pauck, "The Idea of the Church in Christian History," *Church History* 21:3 (1952): 212.

42. Ignatius, *Letter to the Smyrnaeans* 8, my translation. I have rendered the original-language word for *catholic* as "whole" given its particular usage in this context; such a rendering is not uncommon.

43. Polycarp, *Letter to the Philippians* 1, my translation.

44. Gen. 15:13; 1 Chron. 29:15; 1 Peter 1:17; cf. Heb. 11:8 and 1 Peter 1:1.

45. Irenaeus, *Against Heresies* 3.24.1.

46. Tertullian, *On the Exhortation to Chastity* 7, my translation.

47. Origen made these comments in his nonextant commentary on the Song of Solomon, preserved today as fragments in the works of later Christian writers; Origen, *Commentary on the Canticles* 1.1.5 and 2.6.13.

48. Cyprian, *On the Unity of the Whole Church* 5.

49. In saying this, I am not suggesting a Platonic influence or a modern mind-body dualism or anything like this. I am just saying that the emphasis in the fathers was regularly on spiritual things, especially in light of ecclesiology (and eschatology).

50. In very late antiquity, the creed was modified to include "catholic" and "communion of saints" as descriptors of the church.

51. Howard A. Snyder, "The Marks of Evangelical Ecclesiology," in *Evangelical Ecclesiology: Reality or Illusion?* ed. John G. Stackhouse Jr. (Grand Rapids, Mich.: Baker, 2003), 84.

52. Augustine, *The City of God* 16.2.

53. Augustine, *On Faith and Creed* 9.21.

54. Jan Hus, *The Church*, trans. David S. Schaff (New York: Charles Scribner's Sons, 1915), 1 – 4.

55. Martin Luther, *The Smalcald Articles* 3.12.

56. *Augsburg Confession* 7:1.

57. Throughout this book, I will use *sacrament* and *ordinance* interchangeably, though I recognize that different traditions use these words differently.

58. John Calvin, *The Necessity of Reforming the Church*, trans. Henry Beveridge (Philadelphia: Presbyterian Board, 1844), 14.

59. Jaroslav Pelikan, *The Christian Tradition: A History of the Development of Doctrine*, vol. 5, *Christian Doctrine and Modern Culture (Since 1700)* (Chicago: University of Chicago Press, 1989), 282.

60. One such scholar from the Orthodox Church is John Zizioulas; see John D. Zizioulas, *Being as Communion: Studies in Personhood and the Church* (Crestwood, NY: St. Vladimir's Seminary Press, 1985).

61. Craig A. Carter, "Karl Barth's Revision of Protestant Ecclesiology," *Perspectives in Religious Studies* 22:1 (1995): 36 – 39.

62. Karl Barth, *Church Dogmatics* 4/1:652.

63. Darrell L. Guder, ed., *Missional Church: A Vision for the Sending of the Church in North America* (Grand Rapids, Mich.: Eerdmans, 1998), 78.

64. Küng, *The Church*, 86.

Chapter 3: A Telepresent People of God

1. Most surveys place church attendance in the UK in this range; for example, see Jacinta Ashworth and Ian Farthing, "Churchgoing in the UK" (Middlesex, UK: Tearfund, 2007).

2. See for example Randolph Kluver and Yanli Chen, "The Church of Fools: Virtual Ritual and Material Faith," *Online-Heidelberg Journal of Religions on the Internet* 3:1 (2008): 129.

3. From the Ship of Fools website, *ship-of-fools.com*.

4. For a similar view, see Thomas S. Kuhn, *The Structure of Scientific Revolutions*, 3rd ed. (Chicago: University of Chicago Press, 1996).

5. Some readers may feel I am inserting a straw-man argument at this point. However, there are two reasons why I don't feel this is the case. First, outside of the sacraments, there is precious little biblical evidence of physical requirements for churches. Second, in writing this book, I had a difficult time finding scholars or Christian leaders who would go on record with strong arguments for or against virtual churches. At least according to the people I spoke with and the blog-post responses I read, 1 Peter 5:14 appears to be one of the more common biblical references used in the refutation of the validity of virtual churches. My hope is this book will help spur further intelligent debate. Cf. Ally Ostrowski, "Cyber Communion: Finding God in the Little Box," *Journal of Religion and Society* 8 (2006): 7.

6. If you Google MUD, you'll usually read that the *d* stands for *dungeon*. However, the *d* actually stands for *DUNGEN*, a reference to the Fortran-based part of the original Zork (1977), which was based on the first widely used multifaceted computer game, called Adventure (1975). Since the creators of the first MUD (1978), Roy Trubshaw and Richard Bartle, were fans of the offline Dungeons and Dragons (and dungeons were also a prominent fea-

ture in Adventure), the term multi-user dungeon became the assumed articulation of the acronym MUD.

7. For example, Kluver and Chen, "The Church of Fools," 126.

8. Heidi Campbell, "Congregation of the Disembodied: A Look at Religious Community on the Internet," in *Virtual Morality: Morals, Ethics, and New Media*, ed. Mark J. P. Wolf (New York: Peter Lang, 2003), 196.

9. Stephen Shields, "The Legitimacy and Limits of Online Relationships," in *Voices of the Virtual World: Participative Technology and the Ecclesial Revolution*, ed. Leonard Hjalmarson and John La Grou (Wikiklesia, 2007), 307.

10. Raised and educated in the West, I learned a variety of viewpoints about the way the world works from a distinctly Western standpoint. As a Western-oriented pastor to an educated, middle-class, Eastern-oriented congregation, it has been a challenge at times to overcome several foundational differences in viewpoints on issues such as family life, manners of communication, and community organization.

11. Readers may wonder whether Descartes' most famous aphorism contradicts my arguments about virtual community. It doesn't; it actually proves it. Here's why: Descartes' aphorism is a statement on reality. In his mind, what makes a person "real" is the ability to think. Later, Descartes discusses not what makes us real but how we can know. He concludes that it is our minds that prove we are real but it is our bodies that allow us to know. Some thinkers who followed after Descartes went so far as to say that it is *solely* our minds that make us real but it is *solely* our bodies that allow us to know. The challenge with reading Descartes is that he is foremost a thinker; his most substantial contributions to Western philosophy are literally his "meditations," ruminations on a variety of philosophical issues.

12. Descartes was not the originator of this idea (dualism extends back to very early Greek philosophy), but he is the one who established it as a part of the modern philosophical construct.

13. A better way of saying this is that these people had access to the perception of their senses through their minds (as if in a dream). Descartes' differentiation here may sound unusual to twenty-first-century readers because of the stratification of Descartes' thought over the last four centuries.

14. René Descartes, *Meditations on First Philosophy: With Selections from the Objections and Replies*, trans. Michael Moriarty (Oxford: Oxford University Press, 2008).

15. This is not to say that Descartes' view of objective and subjective information is not useful, but as an example, it was used repeatedly by later skeptics to argue that faith and experience of God are subjective and hence are not as real as objective truth.

16. Giuseppe Mantovani and Giuseppe Riva, " 'Real Presence': How Different Ontologies Generate Different Criteria for Presence, Telepresence, and Virtual Presence," *Presence* 8:5 (1999): 542.

17. Anyone who has ever shared the gospel with or tried to disciple an edu-cated, Western individual knows this to be true; the individual resists and struggles with the idea of a "real" spiritual experience or encounter with God. In many ways, modern Western Christians begin their new lives hin-dered in experiencing the movement of God by their rigid and, at times, impoverished, learned viewpoint. (I'm not against the Western worldview, per se; I'm just pointing out its limitations.)

18. Does the Bible define presence? Probably not. The Bible spends very little time on most areas of interest to human philosophy (or, we may better say, the Bible is interested in its own philosophical issues, such as wisdom). Nevertheless, the Bible does reject the modern Western idea that presence is strictly physical. (For example, consider the whole book of Revelation.) Church history rejects this idea too, especially if we con-sider the debates over the presence of the body and blood of Jesus in the Eucharist.

19. Of course, this is an incredibly abbreviated discussion of the nature of presence in modern Western philosophy; space does not allow for interaction with thinkers from Immanuel Kant to John Locke to Martin Heidegger.

20. Cf. Patrick Dixon, *Cyberchurch: Christianity and the Internet* (Eastbourne, UK: Kingsway, 1997), 90–92.

21. Again, if you talk to Westerners, they all want to "touch" God to know that he is "real."

22. Luciano Floridi, "The Philosophy of Presence: From Epistemic Failure to Successful Observation," *Presence* 14:6 (2005): 658.

23. Marie-Laure Ryan, *Narrative as Virtual Reality: Immersion and Interactivity in Literature and Electronic Media* (Baltimore: Johns Hopkins, 2001), 71.

24. Hans Küng, *The Church* (New York: Sheed and Ward, 1967), 84.

25. *Oxford Dictionary and Thesaurus: American Edition* (Oxford: Oxford Univer-sity Press, 1996), 880.

26. Again, this is largely because of Descartes and other modern philosophers and their philosophical constructs.

27. Darrell L. Guder, ed., *Missional Church: A Vision for the Sending of the Church in North America* (Grand Rapids, Mich.: Eerdmans, 1998), 80.

28. By this I mean the geographical where, not where in the sense of the church showing up to do ministry in its community.

29. W. D. Davies, *The Gospel and the Land: Early Christianity and Jewish Territorial Doctrine* (Berkeley: University of California Press, 1974), 336.

30. The writings of the early church fathers also contain many similar refer-ences to individual churches in a single city or region.

31. John S. Hammett, *Biblical Foundations for Baptist Churches: A Contemporary Ecclesiology* (Grand Rapids, Mich.: Kregel, 2005), 29–30.

32. Leo Sang-Min Whang and Geunyoung Chang, "Lifestyles of Virtual World Residents: Living in the On-Line Game 'Lineage,'" *CyberPsychology and Behavior* 7:5 (2004): 592.

33. Walter Brueggemann, *The Land: Place as Gift, Promise and Challenge in Biblical Faith* (Philadelphia: Fortress, 1977), 5. It is interesting to note that open-ended virtual worlds like Second Life have extremely low population densities; it's as if people are so starved for land that they spread out as much as possible once they hit the virtual world. No one wants a cramped apartment or condo in the virtual world; only islands and kingdoms will do.

34. Again, the stories coming from virtual churches such as Church of Fools and St. Pixels testify to this phenomenon.

35. Bob Hyatt, "Technology and the Gospel," in *Voices of the Virtual World: Participative Technology and the Ecclesial Revolution*, ed. Leonard Hjalmarson and John La Grou (Wikiklesia, 2007), 133; and Dixon, *Cyberchurch*, 78.

36. Douglas Groothuis, *The Soul in Cyberspace* (Grand Rapids, Mich.: Baker, 1997), 125–26.

37. I believe these assumptions and criticisms come from a strange mix of apocalyptic millennialism, anti-industrialization, antiurbanization, and Platonic idealism that one finds in North American pseudotheology.

38. Cf. John Palfrey and Urs Gasser, *Born Digital: Understanding the First Generation of Digital Natives* (New York: Basic, 2008), 18.

39. On growing in community, Christians attending virtual churches: see Campbell, "Congregation of the Disembodied," 196. On growing in community, regular people in local networked neighborhoods: see Keith N. Hampton and Barry Wellman, "Examining Community in the Digital Neighborhood: Early Results from Canada's Wired Suburb," in *The Wired Homestead: An MIT Press Sourcebook on the Internet and the Family*, ed. Joseph Turow and Andrea L. Kavanaugh (Cambridge, Mass.: MIT, 2003), 470–72. On not growing in community, gamers with virtual addictions: see Leo Sang-Min Whang, Sujin Lee, and Geunyoung Chang, "Internet Over-Users' Psychological Profiles: A Behavior Sampling Analysis on Internet Addiction," *CyberPsychology and Behavior* 6:2 (2003): 143–50. Contrary to conventional wisdom, evidence suggests that the virtual world often enhances many forms of healthy community.

40. Groothuis, *The Soul in Cyberspace*, 143.

41. Cheryl Casey, "Virtual Ritual, Real Faith: The Revirtualization of Religious Ritual in Cyberspace," *Online-Heidelberg Journal of Religions on the Internet* 2:1 (2006): 85.

42. A growing trend in virtual worlds is the use of bots (automated avatars) to handle mundane community tasks. One church in Second Life I visited used a bot as a greeter!

43. Heidi Campbell, "Living as the Networked People of God," in *Voices of the Virtual World: Participative Technology and the Ecclesial Revolution*, ed. Leonard Hjalmarson and John La Grou (Wikiklesia, 2007), 46.

Chapter 4: The Incarnational Avatar

1. John Smart, Jamais Cascio, and Jerry Paffendorf, "Metaverse Roadmap: Pathways to the 3D Web: A Cross-Industry Public Foresight Project," (unpublished paper, 2007): 6.

2. These layers exist in the real world too, but we are so used to them that they seem like parts of ourselves. An example would be our sense of privacy and disclosure.

3. Mark Stephen Meadows, I, Avatar: The Culture and Consequences of Having a Second Life (Berkeley, Calif.: New Riders, 2008), 66. LifeChurch.tv is also working on an on-the-fly thirty-two-language translator for their virtual worship services.

4. Pablo Martinez-Zárate, Isabela Corduneanu, and Luis Miguel Martinez, "S(L)Pirituality: Immersive Worlds as a Window to Spirituality Phenomena," Online-Heidelberg Journal of Religions on the Internet 3:1 (2008): 213; and cf. Lisa Nakamura, Cybertypes: Race, Ethnicity, and Identity on the Internet (New York: Routledge, 2002): 153.

5. This statement (perhaps this whole chapter) may seem unusual to readers who have never ventured into newer forms of the virtual world. However, as I went through the avatar-creation, training, and learning phases, my avatar's identity just naturally took shape. Of course, it's a projected identity: my cat, Sitka, has a highly developed personality that even includes playing fetch when he's in the right mood, but of course, it is just a personality that I project on an animal that acts instinctively.

6. William Gibson, Neuromancer (New York: Ace, 1984), 16.

7. I use the word encased loosely, and certainly not theologically.

8. Beatrice Bittarello, "Another Time, Another Space: Virtual Worlds, Myth, and Imagination," Online-Heidelberg Journal of Religions on the Internet 3:1 (2008): 260.

9. Tim Hutchings, "Theology and the Online Church," Epworth Review 35:1 (2008).

10. Peter Nagel, "Gnosis, Gnosticism," in The Encyclopedia of Christianity, 4 vols., ed. Erwin Fahlbusch et al., trans. Geoffrey W. Bromiley (Grand Rapids, Mich.: Eerdmans; Leiden: Brill, 2001): 2:417–21.

11. Cf. Douglas Groothuis, "Screwtape Writes Again: Education, for Hell's Sake," The Constructive Curmudgeon blog, May 3, 2008, theconstructivemudgeon.blogspot.com.

12. For some biblical passages that deal with a theology of personhood, please see Eph. 2:1–10 and Heb. 10:22 (inferior body and heart/mind); Matt. 10:28 (body and soul have different properties, but both are subject to God's rule); Luke 12:23 and Rom. 12:1 (importance of the body). I personally do not believe one can develop a taxonomy of personhood based on the Bible.

13. Udo Schnelle, The Human Condition: Anthropology in the Teachings of Jesus, Paul, and John, trans. O. C. Dean Jr. (Minneapolis: Fortress, 1996), 145.

14. Of course, we do strive to engage their bodies in more than worship; this is just an example.

15. This is because of issues regarding personhood and identity formation. As we create identities (or new identities) in the virtual world, it is possible for our identities to seep in one direction or another. For example, if a Second Life Satanist possesses a Satanist avatar, it seems unlikely to result in any type of conversion or spiritual growth. However, if a Satanist chooses to act as a Christian through a Christ-follower avatar, it is possible for the avatar-identity to seep into the identity of the Satanist in the real world (unlikely, perhaps, but possible). Think of it as the people we read about from time to time who are so anti-Christ that they immerse themselves in the Bible and eventually become Christ-followers; it is a related dynamic.

16. There will always be people with different values systems, and so there will always be exceptions.

17. Mark Howe, a member of the management team at St. Pixels, writes about debates that ensued over "avatars' rights" and avatar usage during the Church of Fools experiment; see Mark Howe, "Towards a Theology of Virtual Christian Community" (master's thesis, Spurgeon's College, 2005), 55. Some thinkers have already drafted a formal statement on the rights of avatars; see Raph Koster, "A Declaration of the Rights of Avatars," in *The Second Life Herald: The Virtual Tabloid That Witnessed the Dawn of the Metaverse*, ed. Peter Ludlow and Mark Wallace (Cambridge, Mass.: MIT, 2007), 269 – 73.

18. I asked one avid World of Warcraft player if he played the game as a night elf, and he immediately responded, "What?! No! C'mon, man, a night elf??? You're kidding, right?"

19. Meadows, *I, Avatar*, 50.

20. We know this to be true biblically: God created people with a clear identity (Gen. 1:26 – 27), but sin causes brokenness and anxiety in identity (1 Cor. 13:12; 1 Peter 2:10; and cf. 1 Cor. 5:6).

21. Smart, Cascio, and Paffendorf, "Metaverse Roadmap," 14.

22. Even if Amazon is not around then, they can always use the Wayback search to access the information.

23. Cf. Leo Sang-Min Whang and Geunyoung Chang, "Lifestyles of Virtual World Residents: Living in the On-Line Game 'Lineage,'" *CyberPsychology and Behavior* 7:5 (2004): 599.

24. Andreé Robinson-Neal, "Enhancing the Spiritual Relationship: The Impact of Virtual Worship on the Real World Church Experience," *Online-Heidelberg–Journal of Religions on the Internet* 3:1 (2008): 237.

25. Bobby Gruenewald, "Why Second Life? (Part 1)," *Swerve* blog, ed. Craig Groeschel and Bobby Gruenewald, March 28, 2007, *swerve.lifechurch.tv*.

26. Martinez-Zárate, Corduneanu, and Martinez, "S(L)Pirituality," 218.

27. Think about this: if a person who was born on a deserted island and doesn't know anything about God suddenly has access to a hundred randomly picked church websites, how discipled could that person become?

Answer: they would learn a lot about what programs churches offer, but they would not become very discipled.

28. These two types are not antithetical but are apples and oranges.

29. I-church has a distinctly anti-attractional model for virtual church, which makes it quite distinct from, for example, almost all internet campuses. To me, this type of variety and conversation serves to demonstrate that virtual churches are simply real churches meeting in synthetic space.

30. Rena M. Palloff and Keith Pratt, *Building Online Learning Communities: Effective Strategies for the Virtual Classroom* (San Francisco: Jossey-Bass, 2007), 90.

31. Jeremy N. Bailenson and Andrew C. Beall, "Transformed Social Interaction: Exploring the Digital Plasticity of Avatars," in *Avatars at Work and Play: Collaboration and Interaction in Shared Virtual Environments*, ed. Ralph Schroeder and Ann-Sofie Axelsson (Dordrecht: Springer, 2006), 144.

Chapter 5: WikiWorship

1. In contrast, Lighthouse Church in Second Life chose an unusual bubble-in-the-sky architecture, but at this point, this is clearly not the norm.

2. Brenda E. Brasher, *Give Me That Online Religion* (San Francisco: Jossey-Bass, 2001), 155.

3. Unless God decides to do just that, again.

4. Perhaps a good example is the ritual complexities in Hinduism and Islam. The exception is the many New Age–type sects such as Wicca or the Hare Krishnas. For a variety of sociophilosophical reasons, groups like these have fully adapted their ideologies to virtual worlds.

5. John Calvin, *Institutes of the Christian Religion*, ed. John T. McNeill, trans. Ford Lewis Battles (Philadelphia: Westminster, 1960): 4.17.18.

6. Brasher, *Give Me That Online Religion*, 43.

7. If anything, the concern may be testimonies with "too much information."

8. Pam Smith, priest in charge of i-church, in discussion with the author, August 2008.

9. This is even more important when the prayer request is difficult to mention face-to-face; the feeling of anonymity on the internet probably encourages more honest prayer requests than may be possible in most real-world situations.

10. Kathy T. Hettinga, "Grave Images: A Faith Visualized in a Technological Age," in *Virtual Morality: Morals, Ethics, and New Media*, ed. Mark J. P. Wolf (New York: Peter Lang, 2003), 254.

11. At their website, *www.goarch.org*.

12. As of 2005, the Roman Catholic Church has denied the possibility of Communion online for its members; see Randolph Kluver and Yanli Chen, "The Church of Fools: Virtual Ritual and Material Faith," *Online-Heidelberg Journal of Religions on the Internet* 3:1 (2008): 119.

13. Because of space limitations, we'll discuss only the two most universally accepted Christian ordinances. Traditionally, Roman Catholicism affirms seven sacraments, each of which seems possible for virtual churches to administer. Additionally, footwashing, a practice upheld by a few Christian traditions, is probably possible for virtual churches in a manner similar to Communion or baptism.

14. Tertullian, *The Chaplet* 3.

15. For example, John Howard Yoder, "Sacrament as Social Process: Christ the Transformer of Culture," *Theology Today* 48:1 (1991): 37.

16. For example, Curtis Freeman, "Where Two or Three Are Gathered: Communion Ecclesiology in the Free Church," *Perspectives in Religious Studies* 31:3 (2004): 264–67; and Roger Haight, *Christian Community in History: Historical Ecclesiology* (New York: Continuum, 2004), 98–99.

17. As a result, I don't believe that any one tradition is "correct" in their observance of the Lord's Supper, though there are traditions that appear less convincing than others in the way they practice Communion.

18. It is interesting to note that the New Testament doesn't mention the Lord's Supper at all outside of the Gospels, Acts, and 1 Corinthians.

19. Or for a variety of other reasons all related to traditions of the practice of Communion. A survey of virtual-church participants in 2006 found that about half believe virtual Communion is "sacrilegious"; see Ally Ostrowski, "Cyber Communion: Finding God in the Little Box," *Journal of Religion and Society* 8 (2006): 5. I would argue this is mostly because of a lack of understanding of what Communion is and how it can integrate with technology.

20. For example, in the first centuries AD, followers of the Docetist heresy avoided Communion; see Ignatius, *Letter to the Smyrnaeans* 7. In saying this, it is important to remember that schismatic groups such as the Docetists were not heretical because of their position on Communion; instead, their heresy led to the rejection of Communion. The most notable nonschismatic group that doesn't observe Communion is the Salvation Army. Several virtual-church proponents point to the Salvation Army for support in abstaining from Communion, but this too is a mistake; the Salvation Army does not partake in the Lord's Supper for theological reasons *inherent in its tradition*, not because they are unsure how to administer it. Since virtual churches originate within traditions that administer Communion, these churches must find a way to make virtual Communion a reality for their people.

21. Thomas à Kempis, *The Imitation of Christ* 4.10.

22. To avoid this, virtual churches that prefer this type of virtual Communion could offer designated times, with forum counters that serve to let visitors know that other people are taking Communion with them, so that it is a communal, not an individual, practice.

23. Since I'm not a strong sacramentalist, I don't feel that a priest must administer the elements. Even liturgical theologians can admit the New

Testament doesn't sponsor priestly administration; see Haight, *Christian Community in History*, 121.

24. Because of several textual and exegetical issues, most scholars do not believe 1 Cor. 7:5 refers to fasting. Fasting specifically means to "go hungry" for spiritual reasons.

25. Technically, the telepresent and extensional practice of sacraments are different, though related, approaches. In virtual churches, the ordinances are virtually extended to the recipients, but in augmented churches in the future, the administrator of the sacraments will be telepresent with the recipients. Thus they represent two sides of the same coin.

26. Some sacramental Christians feel very strongly that an important part of Communion is the practice of administering the elements as flesh from flesh, meaning that very real elements are held and offered in very real hands; see Mary Timothy Prokes, *At the Interface: Theology and Virtual Reality* (Tucson: Fenestra, 2004), 64.

27. Justin Martyr, *Apology* 1.67; and Cyprian, *Letters* 2:3.

28. Cyprian, *On the Lapsed* 26; and Tertullian, *On Prayer* 19.

29. For example, Roman Catholicism has the Benediction of the Blessed Sacrament, and Anglicanism has its Office for the Communion of the Sick.

30. Among other things, the Council of Constance (1414–18) tried unsuccessfully to solve papal power grabs, prevented laypeople from taking the cup of Communion in most circumstances, and was responsible for sealing the fate of protoreformer Jan Hus, who was betrayed by a promise of safe transit and burned at the stake.

31. As a proponent of the Free Church model, I really struggle with those who claim that only certain people in the hierarchy can properly administer Communion. It's impossible to defend that position from the Bible. This is the argument made in a number of Reformed blogs to refute the validity of online churches and Communion — ironic, because this is what some of the original Reformers were fighting against.

32. See also Ps. 51:7.

33. Hans Küng, *The Church* (New York: Sheed and Ward, 1967), 205.

34. In the original language of Matthew 3, confession is not something that occurs prior to baptism but is presented as an ongoing act coinciding with baptism.

35. Küng, *The Church*, 209; and Jonathan R. Wilson, *Why Church Matters: Worship, Ministry, and Mission in Practice* (Grand Rapids, Mich.: Brazos, 2006), 106.

36. The *Didache* is an early Christian document, though in a few places (such as chapters 6 and 8), it diverges from some of Paul's ideas. It is possible it was a rudimentary document circulated to explain church practices, possibly without the author's being fully conversant in what we now call the New Testament. It is also quite likely that the original document reflects the mindset of first-century Christians.

37. As a dunker myself, it is interesting to note that the *Didache* recommends baptism in cold "living" water, meaning that it prioritizes running water over a pool before it prioritizes immersion over pouring.
38. Tertullian, *On Baptism* 4.
39. Mike and Sally Williams, thirty-year career missionaries to Muslims, in discussion with the author, October 2008.
40. Special thanks to Brian Vasil at Flamingo Road for the use of *outsourced* in this way.
41. Brian Vasil, Flamingo Road Internet Campus Pastor, in discussion with the author, September 2008.
42. Pastors know that peer pressure to take Communion is always a big problem in real-world churches, but it seems that virtual Communion could minimize this greatly.
43. Cheryl Casey, "Virtual Ritual, Real Faith: The Revirtualization of Religious Ritual in Cyberspace," *Online-Heidelberg Journal of Religions on the Internet* 2:1 (2006): 85.
44. Heidi Campbell, "Living as the Networked People of God," in *Voices of the Virtual World: Participative Technology and the Ecclesial Revolution*, ed. Leonard Hjalmarson and John La Grou (Wikiklesia, 2007), 48.

Chapter 6: Almighty Mod

1. I'm happy to report that Cameron remains active in ministry at BVC to this day.
2. Kerstin Radde-Antweiler, "Virtual Religion: An Approach to a Religious and Ritual Topography of Second Life," *Online-Heidelberg Journal of Religions on the Internet* 3:1 (2008): 188.
3. Heidi Campbell, "Who's Got the Power? Religious Authority and the Internet," *Journal of Computer-Mediated Communication* 12:3 (2007).
4. In other words, they argue that if you buy a car and tinker under the hood, that's your right because you own the car. Many tech companies believe you should buy their product but not be allowed to tinker under the hood; great examples include Microsoft's Windows Vista and Apple's iPhone.
5. As an example, Tim Guest cites a person banned from Second Life for creating a Confederate-flag-waving KKK avatar. Offensive for sure, but Second Life has lots of other offensive avatars. What about them? As a journalist, Guest documents the capricious approach to ethics employed by Linden Lab, developer of Second Life. Similarly, Tom Boellstorff writes that a big issue facing the virtual world is the possibility of "virtual dictatorships." I contacted Linden Lab to talk about this issue, but they did not respond to my request for an interview. See Tim Guest, *Second Lives: A Journey through Virtual Worlds* (New York: Random House, 2007), 110–12; and Tom Boellstorff, *Coming of Age in Second Life: An Anthropologist Explores the Virtually Human* (Princeton, N.J.: Princeton University Press, 2008), 222.

6. Mark Howe, a member of the management team of St. Pixels, admits their church's leadership is often akin to a "benign dictatorship"; see Mark Howe, *Online Church? First Steps towards Virtual Incarnation* (Ridley Hall, UK: Grove, 2007), 13.

7. The virtual world is likely to be as much a game-changer in the area of authority as was the printing press and the Roman road system.

8. Brasher, *Give Me That Online Religion*, 42.

9. Ignatius, the first-century bishop of Antioch, would definitely consider it unhealthy; see Ignatius, *Letter to the Smyrnaeans* 9.

10. If a Presbyterian body objected, the owner could move the account offshore, and the church would be unstoppable.

11. What makes a pastor "real" anyway? As we can see, the new virtual world regularly hits really old nerves in the working out of the idea of church.

12. Christopher Helland explains it best: there are "these magnificent sites, and often people would think, well, because it's a good-looking site, and it's very user friendly, and it's beautiful, it must be authentic, it must be real, this guy must be a real religious expert, but really, no, they're not, they're a twelve-year-old kid"; see Christopher Helland, "Turning Cyberspace into Sacred Space: Examining the Religious Revolution Occurring on the World Wide Web," Google TechTalks, May 31, 2007, *youtube.com*.

13. Radde-Antweiler, "Virtual Religion," 204.

14. Brother Maynard, "Hyperlinks Subvert Hierarchy: The Internet, Non-Hierarchical Organizations, and the Structure of the Church," in *Voices of the Virtual World: Participative Technology and the Ecclesial Revolution*, ed. Leonard Hjalmarson and John La Grou (Wikiklesia, 2007), 175.

15. Patrick Dixon, *Cyberchurch: Christianity and the Internet* (Eastbourne, UK: Kingsway, 1997), 79.

16. Paul S. Minear, *Images of the Church in the New Testament*, New Testament Library (Louisville: Westminster John Knox, 2004), 223.

17. He did have some strange views, like the idea that Jesus and the disciples never consumed wine (contra Matt. 26:27).

18. Maybe the twelve-year-old kid would have proven to be a better pastor than the Silverlake guy!

19. C. Scott Andreas, "A Networked E(-)cclesia: Cultivating Community in an Age of Convergence," in *Voices of the Virtual World: Participative Technology and the Ecclesial Revolution*, ed. Leonard Hjalmarson and John La Grou (Wikiklesia, 2007), 15.

20. A disadvantage of the virtual world is that the legal system hasn't caught up with technology. My real-world church is owned by the church, not by me, but many virtual-world churches appear to be owned by a person, often the pastor.

21. Helland, "Turning Cyberspace into Sacred Space."

22. Pablo Martinez-Zárate, Isabela Corduneanu, and Luis Miguel Martinez, "S(L)Pirituality: Immersive Worlds as a Window to Spirituality Phenomena," *Online-Heidelberg Journal of Religions on the Internet* 3:1 (2008): 215.

23. For example, Lorne L. Dawson and Douglas E. Cowan, *Religion Online: Finding Faith on the Internet* (New York: Routledge, 2004), 3; and Nadja Miczek, "Rituals Online: Dynamic Processes Reflecting Individual Perspectives," *Masaryk University Journal of Law and Technology* 1:2 (2007): 203.

24. John La Grou, "Foreword: Surfing the Liminal Domains," in *Voices of the Virtual World: Participative Technology and the Ecclesial Revolution*, ed. Leonard Hjalmarson and John La Grou (Wikiklesia, 2007), 2.

25. Andrew Jones, "Linking to Cyberchurch," *Relevant*, December 27, 2005, *relevantmagazine.com*.

26. There has been increased interest in challenging the unilateral use of EULAs by software providers; see Peter Ludlow and Mark Wallace, *The Second Life Herald: The Virtual Tabloid That Witnessed the Dawn of the Metaverse* (Cambridge, Mass.: MIT, 2007), 156–57.

27. *Organization* is not the best word to describe a church, but even a radically decentralized church of equals still behaves as such because it has someone or some group that makes decisions, even if it is only choosing what questions to ask.

28. The founder of Second Life is on record as saying that Second Life eliminates the need for God; see Wagner James Au, *The Making of Second Life: Notes from the New World* (New York: HarperCollins, 2008), 234.

29. Boellstorff, *Coming of Age in Second Life*, 236.

30. Bobby Gruenewald, Innovation Pastor at LifeChurch.tv, in discussion with the author, August 2008. He also sees the potential benefit of an organization like the Evangelical Council of Financial Accountability, as do several other leaders affiliated with virtual churches.

31. Patricia Wallace, *The Psychology of the Internet* (Cambridge: Cambridge University Press, 1999), 61.

32. For example, Daniel J. Solove, *The Future of Reputation: Gossip, Rumor, and Privacy on the Internet* (New Haven, Conn.: Yale University Press, 2007), 142–46.

33. Augustine, *Commentary on the Psalms* 120:1–2.

34. Rex Miller, "Digital Immigrants Go Native," in *Voices of the Virtual World: Participative Technology and the Ecclesial Revolution*, ed. Leonard Hjalmarson and John La Grou (Wikiklesia, 2007), 205.

Chapter 7: Synthetic Sin

1. Griefers, ragers, and trolls are loose monikers for inhabitants of the virtual world who don't like to play nice with the other inhabitants. A *griefer* is someone who enters a virtual world for the purpose of harassing people or causing them grief through insults, attacks, stalking, or manipulation of the virtual world's system. A *rager* is a person who aggressively attacks

other people and the virtual world system with the intent of destroying both. They can act very irrationally when dealt with. A *troll* is someone who says or posts highly inflammatory statements to provoke people. Often trolls lie in wait or skulk around high-traffic areas of virtual worlds (or other internet phenomena such as blogs) to post their offensive content over and over again. The word *troll* comes more from the fishing idea of trolling (dragging bait slowly through the water to catch unsuspecting fish) than from the mythological creature.

2. As we remember, the Bible explains sin as the human failing of people; sin is our brokenness, which entered humanity in the garden and causes us to live selfish, hurting, I-don't-need-God kinds of lives (Rom. 3:23).

3. In other words, in places like China, owners of virtual businesses hire real poor people at low wages to sit at computers and create virtual clothing for rich people to purchase for their avatars. In the much more lucrative gaming world, the poor people at the computer terminals take control of rich people's virtual warriors and do small repetitive tasks thousands and thousands of times to level-up the warriors, and then the business owners sell the warriors back to the rich people; see Tim Guest, *Second Lives: A Journey through Virtual Worlds* (New York: Random House, 2007), 8.

4. Stephen Hutcheon, "Anshe's Kinky Past Revealed," *Sydney Morning Herald*, January 17, 2007.

5. Peter Ludlow and Mark Wallace, *The Second Life Herald: The Virtual Tabloid That Witnessed the Dawn of the Metaverse* (Cambridge, Mass.: MIT, 2007), 104.

6. Guest, *Second Lives*, 66 – 69.

7. For the survivors' group incident, see Tom Boellstorff, *Coming of Age in Second Life: An Anthropologist Explores the Virtually Human* (Princeton, N.J.: Princeton University Press, 2008), 189.

8. Guest, *Second Lives*, 9.

9. Julian Dibbell, "A Rape in Cyberspace," in *Flame Wars: The Discourse of Cyberculture*, ed. Mark Dery (Durham, N.C.: Duke University Press, 1997), 237 – 61.

10. Randolph Kluver and Yanli Chen, "The Church of Fools: Virtual Ritual and Material Faith," *Online-Heidelberg Journal of Religions on the Internet* 3:1 (2008): 123.

11. Ludlow and Wallace, *The Second Life Herald*.

12. Cf. John Smart, Jamais Cascio, and Jerry Paffendorf, "Metaverse Roadmap: Pathways to the 3D Web: A Cross-Industry Public Foresight Project," (2007): 23.

13. In practice, EULAs and TOSs are loosely defined, and so the comparison I make will not always be applicable to every EULA or TOS.

14. The police could cite me for disturbing the peace, but I would have a legal right to defend myself, unlike in many virtual worlds.

15. It's interesting because MMORPGs have codes or a teleology built into their worlds which makes them feel very different from open virtual worlds such as Second Life.

16. Mary Prokes argues that people's choosing to be disembodied, not the pull of free agency, is what causes a greater tendency toward sinfulness, but this cannot be true; otherwise we would expect to see similar problems with the use of the telephone; see Mary Timothy Prokes, *At the Interface: Theology and Virtual Reality* (Tucson, Ariz.: Fenestra, 2004), 38.

17. Pope John Paul II, *Veritatis Splendor*, 31 – 32.

18. John Palfrey and Urs Gasser, *Born Digital: Understanding the First Generation of Digital Natives* (New York: Basic, 2008), 91, 97; and Boellstorff, *Coming of Age in Second Life*, 187.

19. Cf. Scott Ragan and John Sexton, "Visible Church for an Invisible World," in *Voices of the Virtual World: Participative Technology and the Ecclesial Revolution*, ed. Leonard Hjalmarson and John La Grou (Wikiklesia, 2007), 264.

20. Ludlow and Wallace, *The Second Life Herald*, 92.

21. Two separate studies document this. See Nick Yee, Jeremy N. Bailenson, Mark Urbanek, Francis Chang, and Dan Merget, "The Unbearable Lightness of Being Digital: The Persistence of Nonverbal Social Norms in Online Virtual Environments," *CyberPsychology and Behavior* 10:1 (2007): 115 – 21; and Boellstorff, *Coming of Age in Second Life*, 149.

22. Brenda E. Brasher, *Give Me That Online Religion* (San Francisco: Jossey-Bass, 2001), 100.

23. Mark Stephen Meadows, *I, Avatar: The Culture and Consequences of Having a Second Life* (Berkeley, Calif.: New Riders, 2008), 78.

24. Again, without naming names, my research reveals this is the biggest reason why church leaders won't engage the virtual world head-on — they don't believe it's real, mostly because they're not a part of it.

25. Brasher, *Give Me That Online Religion*, 95.

26. Already anecdotal evidence suggests many, if not most, people think virtual sex with someone other than their spouse is not sinful; it's not extramarital sex because it's not "real" sex.

27. Maura McCarthy argues convincingly that an uncensored internet is better for churches; a censored internet will most likely censor churches as well; see Maura McCarthy, "Free Market Morality: Why Evangelicals Need Free Speech on the Internet," in *Virtual Morality: Morals, Ethics, and New Media*, ed. Mark J. P. Wolf (New York: Peter Lang, 2003), 217.

28. Again, proclamation gets us only halfway. We need more than content; we need context (Acts 8:31).

29. Here I'm using the word *sanctify* in the biblical, not the theological, sense. Biblically, *to sanctify* means to make holy, and the term can be applied to people, places, or things. Theologically, *to sanctify* is often used as shorthand for the change that believers make to become more like God.

30. "Human relationships are aided by the consensual misremembering of slights, allowing the sting of insults and personal offenses to fade over time. With easy access to records of past wrongs, 'I forgot,' will be much less frequent, and some will find it impossible to 'let bygones be bygones'" (Smart, Cascio, and Paffendorf, "Metaverse Roadmap," 15).

31. Daniel J. Solove, *The Future of Reputation: Gossip, Rumor, and Privacy on the Internet* (New Haven, Conn.: Yale University Press, 2007), 4.

32. Some might suggest that he could "hide" better in the virtual world, but this is not really true; it's not as if he announces his past when he comes to our church, nor would we want him to do that, for his sake. His legal status forces him to make decisions about what he reveals about himself, whether in the virtual world or the real world, since his convictions are logged for anyone to see.

33. In the real world, it would be awkward and just plain weird for a person to walk around with a sign saying, "Hi, I'm Fred. One thing you'll learn about me is that when I was younger, I did a lot of stupid and bad things that landed me in prison. While there I found Jesus and he has forgiven me for those stupid, bad things I did. By his grace, I am redeemed." In the virtual world? Perfectly natural in his profile.

34. "Perhaps the most obvious persistent trend [in virtual worlds] will be identity experimentation, self-revelation and role play in VWs, and the creative variation of social norms around gender, ethnicity, social class, etiquette, and group values and goals. We see this in today's pioneering social VWs like Second Life, and social networks like MySpace. As the virtual worlds scenario unfolds, we can expect an explosion in the number of people engaged in such activities, and the ensuing social change to bring both positive and disruptive effects." The authors of this study also see a future with both validated and anonymous worlds; see Smart, Cascio, and Paffendorf, "Metaverse Roadmap," 8.

35. Douglas Groothuis, *The Soul in Cyberspace* (Grand Rapids, Mich.: Baker, 1997), 41.

36. It's also probably not true in general. Very few people can truly disguise themselves in the virtual world better than they can in the real world; there are resources that allow for identity discovery. See Robert Jones, *Internet Forensics* (Sebastopol: O'Reilly, 2006); and for a contrast of the agrarian, industrial, and digital ages of anonymity, see Palfrey and Gasser, *Born Digital*, 17–20.

37. The reason? People have been perfecting real-world masks for thousands of years.

38. Pablo Martinez-Zárate, Isabela Corduneanu, and Luis Miguel Martinez, "S(L)Pirituality: Immersive Worlds as a Window to Spirituality Phenomena," *Online-Heidelberg Journal of Religions on the Internet* 3:1 (2008): 220.

39. Unknowingly, when I created my avatar in Second Life, I did this very thing, and my wife gave me a hard time. Yet it's a lot easier to create a beautiful avatar in Second Life than an ugly one.

40. We could argue motive, perhaps, but that's a slippery slope, in that my motive for picking a handsome avatar for myself could be much more fiendish than a male friend's motive for picking a female robot for his avatar — though church culture probably would judge him more harshly. The issue of motive is problematic for the church in both the real world and the virtual world.

41. Though I doubt a person can ever be completely free of masks in this lifetime (cf. Rom. 3:11 – 12).

42. Mark Brown, priest in charge of the Anglican Cathedral in Second Life, in discussion with the author, July 2008.

43. Stefano Pace, "Miracles or Love? How Religious Leaders Communicate Trustworthiness through the Web," *Journal of Religion and Popular Culture* 7 (2004): 20.

44. Groothuis, *The Soul in Cyberspace*, 35.

Chapter 8: The Internet Campus

1. Granted, the company I worked for provided sensitive testing services to law enforcement agencies. They used the tests I ran in the prosecution of criminal cases.

2. In my view of the church, this would include Titus 1:6 – 9, for example.

3. Brian Vasil, Internet Campus Pastor at Flamingo Road Church, in discussion with the author, September 2008.

4. As Vasil notes, a church can always hire someone to handle the technology (just as churches hire companies to print materials, repair buildings, or even build websites), but a church can't outsource virtual ministry any more than it can outsource traditional ministry.

5. One of the greatest enemies of the kingdom of God is misunderstanding, and everything accompanying it, from the inability to forgive to pride to hardheartedness (Eph. 4:31 – 32; Matt. 6:14).

6. Of course, this is not what virtual-church pastors actually do, but this is the perception many people may have.

7. We'll talk about this more in chapter 10.

8. Jonathan R. Wilson, *Why Church Matters: Worship, Ministry, and Mission in Practice* (Grand Rapids, Mich.: Brazos, 2006), 96 – 99.

9. Jesus' statement on discipline is unique in that it is one of the few (maybe the only) recorded references made by Jesus about the church, but it is somewhat common in that it closely follows ancient Jewish tradition practiced in the synagogue (and taught by rabbis, not to mention the Qumran community).

10. Wilson, *Why Church Matters*, 96 – 99.

11. Some virtual, non-Christian religious communities have systems whereby different people are allowed different avatar attachments (such as halos) based on the person's level of commitment and place in the organization. The goal is to differentiate the leaders from the followers, but if a church

did this, would it separate the leaders from the followers, or the sheep from the goats? Both? Neither?

Chapter 9: Viral Ministry

1. There is a great deal of debate as to what the value of each of these networks becomes.
2. David P. Reed, "That Sneaky Exponential: Beyond Metcalfe's Law to the Power of Community Building," *Context* (1999).
3. Mary Jacobs, "Family Resemblance: Methodism's Cousins Span Wide Range," *United Methodist Portal* blog (August 2008).
4. Neil Ormerod, "The Structure of a Systematic Ecclesiology," *Theological Studies* 63:1 (2002): 16.
5. Edward Schillebeeckx, *The Church with a Human Face: A New and Expanded Theology of Ministry* (New York: Crossroad, 1985), 83.
6. Nicholas M. Healy, *Church, World and the Christian Life: Practical-Prophetic Ecclesiology* (Cambridge: Cambridge University Press, 2000), 5. In saying this, neither I nor Healy are speaking pragmatically; what I am saying is that when we encounter something that is in its very nature and essence a divine mystery, it can be helpful to understand this something's qualities or properties first, in order to understand its nature. This is the way we study God; we don't try to figure out his nature without first considering his qualities or attributes, such as omniscience, etc.
7. Richard Bliese, "The Mission Matrix: Mapping Out the Complexities of a Missional Ecclesiology," *Word and World* 26:3 (2006): 248.
8. Luther is often credited with this idea, but it's an idea that was held throughout church history; see Wolfhart Pannenberg, *Systematic Theology*, trans. Geoffrey W. Bromiley (Grand Rapids, Mich.: Eerdmans, 1998), 3:125.
9. John S. Hammett, *Biblical Foundations for Baptist Churches: A Contemporary Ecclesiology* (Grand Rapids, Mich.: Kregel, 2005), 46; and see Pannenberg, *Systematic Theology*, 3:125.
10. As I mentioned, of all the virtual churches I spoke with, i-church appears to be the most focused on a social-networking model for church life and ministry. Flamingo Road is also experimenting with some aspects of this.
11. Some of the people I am referring to have testified to their virtual-church pastors regarding their struggles to "fit in" in real-world churches. Obviously, marginal people do attend real-world churches; the point here is to raise big-picture questions.
12. Of course, there is a great margin between those who have computers and those who don't. We'll take this up in the next chapter.
13. While it's beyond the scope of this book, conventional wisdom about people who dress as a member of the opposite sex is inaccurate and misleading. What we can agree on here is that, regardless of what they choose

to wear, they are people just like me and you, God is able to heal and restore them, and God has a purpose for their lives.

14. Heidi Campbell's research shows this is already happening; see Heidi Campbell, *Exploring Religious Community Online: We Are One in the Network*, Digital Formations 24 (New York: Peter Lang, 2005), 139.

15. Studies show that many people who get involved in a virtual church also look to get involved in a real-world church or ministry; see Campbell, *Exploring Religious Community Online*, 162.

16. Real-world pastors understand that there are barriers to limitless growth, such as facilities, population density, and people management. Interestingly enough, virtual churches also encounter caps to growth that they must overcome (Mark Howe, management team member of St. Pixels, in discussion with the author, February 2009).

17. Heidi Campbell, "Congregation of the Disembodied: A Look at Religious Community on the Internet," in *Virtual Morality: Morals, Ethics, and New Media*, ed. Mark J. P. Wolf (New York: Peter Lang, 2003), 189.

18. Brenda E. Brasher, *Give Me That Online Religion* (San Francisco: Jossey-Bass, 2001), 49.

19. I use this as an example because my wife is a marriage and family therapist who works in domestic-violence group counseling. It may seem strange, but running these support groups in the virtual world has some significant advantages (plus a few negatives, of course).

20. Cf. Campbell, "Congregation of the Disembodied," 190.

Chapter 10: The Social-Network Church

1. Even Wesley included a limiter in his statement, which was that the world was his parish insomuch as it was people with whom he had some sort of contact.

2. Heidi Campbell, "Living as the Networked People of God," in *Voices of the Virtual World: Participative Technology and the Ecclesial Revolution*, ed. Leonard Hjalmarson and John La Grou (Wikiklesia, 2007), 48.

3. Gitte Stald, "Outlook and Insight: Young Danes' Uses of the Internet — Navigating Global Seas and Local Waters," in *The Wired Homestead: An MIT Press Sourcebook on the Internet and the Family*, ed. Joseph Turow and Andrea L. Kavanaugh (Cambridge, Mass.: MIT, 2003), 228 – 29.

4. For the record, I am very interested in politics and believe Christians as citizens should be involved in all aspects of civic life, but I think that the priority of the church is to glorify God through the gospel and through people.

5. I don't know if it's possible for any church to avoid this problem; all churches are contextualized — which is a good thing!

6. There is a great deal of debate about the meaning of *neighbor* in the original language; however, we can probably say with some certainty that it doesn't

mean "everyone else in the world," at least in its original context. Cf., Brenda E. Brasher, *Give Me That Online Religion* (San Francisco: Jossey-Bass, 2001), 116.

7. Patricia Wallace, *The Psychology of the Internet* (Cambridge: Cambridge University Press, 1999), 9.

8. John Smart, Jamais Cascio, and Jerry Paffendorf, "Metaverse Roadmap: Pathways to the 3D Web: A Cross-Industry Public Foresight Project," (2007): 19.

9. Jo Guldi, "A Map of the Virtual Territory: Individual, Church, and Society in the Twenty-first Century," in *Voices of the Virtual World: Participative Technology and the Ecclesial Revolution*, ed. Leonard Hjalmarson and John La Grou (Wikiklesia, 2007), 98.

10. John S. Hammett, *Biblical Foundations for Baptist Churches: A Contemporary Ecclesiology* (Grand Rapids, Mich.: Kregel, 2005), 48.

11. Walking around after the service, it did not appear to me that the neighborhood the church is in is predominantly Caucasian.

12. For example, Calvin Park, "Using the Machine," in *Voices of the Virtual World: Participative Technology and the Ecclesial Revolution*, ed. Leonard Hjalmarson and John La Grou (Wikiklesia, 2007), 239.

13. In *I, Avatar*, Mark Meadows tells of a bot (AI avatar) that translates spoken language into sign language; in the future these types of bots may allow non-English speakers to understand English-language churches; see Mark Stephen Meadows, *I, Avatar: The Culture and Consequences of Having a Second Life* (Berkeley, Calif.: New Riders, 2008), 110.

14. Kevin M. Rogers, "The Digital Divide Revisited: The Grand Canyon of the Online Environment?" *Masaryk University Journal of Law and Technology* 1:2 (2007): 157 – 71.

15. Ally Ostrowski, "Cyber Communion: Finding God in the Little Box," *Journal of Religion and Society* 8 (2006): 4.

16. Paul S. Minear, *Images of the Church in the New Testament*, New Testament Library (Louisville: Westminster John Knox, 2004), 143.

17. LifeChurch.tv is one of several churches trying to work out solutions to this impasse; Flamingo Road Church is pursuing a viable virtual youth ministry.

Conclusion: A Church on Every Node

1. Many people think this may be the case; see Brenda E. Brasher, *Give Me That Online Religion* (San Francisco: Jossey-Bass, 2001), 16 – 19.

2. Ibid., 23.

3. One artificial solution to these kinds of issues that pops up every generation is the house church, but thankfully, it needn't be the only solution.

4. Andreé Robinson-Neal, "Enhancing the Spiritual Relationship: The Impact of Virtual Worship on the Real World Church Experience," *Online-Heidelberg Journal of Religions on the Internet* 3:1 (2008): 234.

5. Brasher, *Give Me That Online Religion*, 142.

6. For example, Pam Smith, priest in charge of i-church, in discussion with the author, August 2008; and Heidi Campbell, "Living as the Networked People of God," in *Voices of the Virtual World: Participative Technology and the Ecclesial Revolution*, ed. Leonard Hjalmarson and John La Grou (Wikiklesia, 2007), 49.

7. Paul S. Minear, *Images of the Church in the New Testament*, New Testament Library (Louisville: Westminster John Knox, 2004), 250.

8. Ibid., 72.

9. Patrick Dixon, *Cyberchurch: Christianity and the Internet* (Eastbourne, UK: Kingsway, 1997), 58.

10. Brasher, *Give Me That Online Religion*, 44.

11. Mark Brown, priest in charge of the Anglican Cathedral in Second Life, in discussion with the author, July 2008.

12. Stanley Hauerwas and William H. Willimon, *Resident Aliens: Life in the Christian Colony* (Nashville: Abingdon, 1989), 49.

Index

Written by Douglas Estes